CONSTITUTION,

LAWS,

AND

TREATIES

OF THE

CHICKASAWS,

BY AUTHORITY.

SR Scholarly Resources Inc.
1508 Pennsylvania Avenue · Wilmington, Delaware 19806

SCHOLARLY RESOURCES, INC.
Wilmington, Delaware • London

Reprint edition published in 1975

Library of Congress Catalog Card Number: 75-3675
ISBN: 0-8420-1841-7

Manufactured in the United States of America

CONSTITUTION,

LAWS,

AND

TREATIES

OF THE

CHICKASAWS,

BY AUTHORITY.

TISHOMINGO CITY:
PRINTED BY E. J. FOSTER.
1860.

CONSTITUTION.

WE, the people of the Chickasaw Nation, acknowledging with gratitude the grace and beneficence of GOD, in permitting us to make choice of our own form of Government, do, in accordance with the first, second, fourth and seventh articles of the Treaty between the United States, the Choctaws and Chickasaws, made and concluded at Washington City, June 22d, A. D. 1855, ordain and establish this Constitution for our Government, within the following limits, to wit: Beginning on the north bank of Red River, at the mouth of Island Bayou, where it empties into Red River, about twenty-six miles on a straight line below the mouth of False Washita; thence running a north-westerly course along the main channel of said Bayou to the junction of the Three Prongs of said Bayou nearest the dividing ridge between Washita and Low Blue Rivers, as laid down on Capt. R. L. Hunter's Map; thence northerly along the eastern prong of said Island Bayou to its source; thence due north to the Canadian River; thence west along the main Canadian to the ninety-eighth degree of west longitude; thence south to Red River, and thence down Red River to the beginning; *Provided, however*, if a line running due north from the eastern source of Island Bayou to the main Canadian, shall not include Allen's or Wapa nacka Academy within the Chickasaw District, then an offset shall be made from said line, so as to leave said Academy two miles within the Chickasaw District, north, west and south from the lines of boundary.

ARTICLE 1.

BILL OF RIGHTS.

That the general, great and essential principles of liberty and free government may be recognized and established, we declare that

SEC. 1. All political power is inherent in the people, and all free governments are founded on their authority, and instituted for their benefit; and they have at all times the inalienable right to alter, reform or abolish their form of government in such manner as they may think expedient.

SEC. 2. All freemen, when they form a social compact, have equal rights, and no man or set of men is entitled to exclusive, separate, public emoluments or privileges, but in consideration of public services.

SEC. 3. No religious test shall ever be required as a qualification to any office of public trust in this Nation.

SEC. 4. All men have a natural and indefeasible right to worship God according to the dictates of their own consciences. No man shall be compelled to attend, erect, or support any place of worship, or to maintain any ministry against his consent. No human authority ought, in any case whatever, to control or interfere with the rights of conscience in matters of religion, and no preference shall ever be given by law to any religious society, or mode of worship; but it shall be the duty of the Legislature to pass such laws as shall be necessary to protect every religious denomination in the peaceable enjoyment of their own mode of worship.

SEC. 5. Every citizen shall be at liberty to speak, write, or publish his opinions on any subject, being responsible for the abuse of that privilege: and no law shall ever be passed curtailing the liberty of speech, or of the press.

SEC. 6. The people shall be secure in their persons, houses, papers and possessions, from all unreasonable searches or seizures; and no warrant to search any place, or to seize any thing, shall issue without describing them, as near as may be, nor without probable cause, supported by oath or affirmation; *Provided, however*, that searches for, and seizures of, intoxicating liquors, are not to be considered unreasonable searches or seizures.

Sec. 7. In all criminal prosecutions the accused shall have a speedy public trial, by an impartial jury. He shall not be compelled to give evidence against himself. He shall have the right of being heard by himself or counsel, or both; shall be confronted with the witnesses against him, and shall have compulsory process for obtaining witnesses in his favor. And no person shall be holden to answer for any criminal charge, but on indictment or information.

Sec. 8. All prisoners shall be baleable by sufficient sureties, except such as may, in the opinion of the Judge of the examining court, be guilty of wilful murder.

Sec. 9. Excessive bail shall not be required, nor excessive fines imposed, nor cruel or unusual punishments inflic ted. All courts shall be open; and every person for an injury done him in his lands, goods, person or reputation, shall have remedy by course of law.

Sec. 10. No person, for the same offence, shall be twice put in jeopardy of life or limb; nor shall a person be again put upon trial for the same offence, after a verdict of not guilty. And the right of trial by jury shall remain inviolate.

Sec. 11. The Legislature shall have the power, by law, to prescribe the mode and manner of persons bearing arms in defence of themselves or their country.

Sec. 12. No person shall ever be imprisoned for debt.

Sec. 13. The citizens shall have the right, in a peaceable manner, to assemble together for their common good, and to apply to those invested with powers of government for redress of grievances, or other purposes, by address or remonstrance.

Sec. 14. No power of suspending the laws of this Nation shall be exercised, except by the Legislature or its authority.

Sec. 15. The Legislature shall pass no retrospective law, or any law impairing the obligation of contracts.

SEC. 16. Polygamy shall not be tolerated in this Nation from and after the adoption of this constitution.

ARTICLE 2.

RIGHTS OF SUFFRAGE.

SEC. 1. No idiot, or insane person or persons, convicted of any infamous crime, shall be entitled to the privileges of an elector.

SEC. 2. All elections by the people shall be by *viva voce.*

SEC. 3. All free male persons of the age of nineteen years and upwards, who are by birth or adoption members of the Chickasaw tribe of Indians, who shall have resided six months immediately preceding any election in the Chickasaw Nation, shall be deemed qualified electors; *Provided, however,* That all Chickasaws who desire, shall be entitled to vote in the first general election held in the Chickasaw Nation under the authority of this constitution.

SEC. 4. Electors, in all cases, shall be privileged from arrest during their attendance at elections, in going to, and returning from the same, except in cases of treason, felony, or breach of the peace.

ARTICLE 3.

DIVISION OF THE POWERS OF GOVERNMENT.

SECTION 1. The powers of the government of the Chickasaw Nation shall be divided into three distinct departments, and each of them confided to a separate body of magistracy, to wit: Those which are Legislative to one; those which are Executive to another, and those which are Judicial to another. And no person, or collection of persons, being one of those departments, shall exercise any power properly attached to either of the others, except in the instances herein expressly permitted.

ARTICLE 4.

LEGISLATIVE DEPARTMENT.

SECTION 1. The Legislative powers of this Nation shall be vested in two distinct branches; the one to be styled the Senate, and the other the House of Representatives; and both together, the Legislature of the Chickasaw Nation. The style of the laws shall be: "Be it enacted by the Legislature of the Chickasaw Nation."

SEC. 2. The members of the House of Representatives shall be chosen by the qualified electors, and their term of office shall be one year from the day of the general election. And the session of the Legislature shall be annual, at Tishomingo; commencing on the first Monday in October, in each and every year.

SEC. 3. No person shall be a Representative unless he be a Chickasaw by birth or adoption, and shall have been an inhabitant of the Chickasaw Nation one year next preceding his election, and the last six months thereof a citizen of the county for which he shall be chosen, and shall have attained to the age of twenty-one years at the time of his election.

SEC. 4. The Senators shall be chosen by the qualified electors for the term of two years, at the same time and place as Representatives. And no person shall be a Senator unless he be a Chickasaw by birth or adoption, and have been a citizen of the Chickasaw Nation one year next preceding his election, and the last six months a citizen of the senatorial district for which he shall be chosen, and shall have attained to the age of thirty years at the time of his election.

SEC. 5. The number of Senators shall not be less than one-third nor more than two-thirds of the number of Representatives.

SEC. 6. The Legislature shall have power, by law, to prescribe the mode and manner of enumerating and apportioning the number of inhabitants necessary for the election of Representatives to the Legislature; *Provided, however*, no county shall have less than one Representative until the first enumeration and apportionment by the Legislature. The following shall be the apportionment of Representatives among the several counties, viz: the counties of Pickens and Tishomingo shall elect four Representatives each; the counties of Panola and Pontotoc shall elect five Representatives each.

SEC. 7. The Legislature shall divide the Chickasaw Nation into four senatorial districts; *Provided, however*, until said division, the counties of Panola, Pickens, Tishomingo and Pontotoc shall each respectively constitute a senatorial district. And each senatorial district shall be entitled to elect three Senators.

SEC. 8. The House of Representatives, when assembled, shall choose a Speaker and its other officers, and the Senate shall choose a President and its officers. And each House shall judge of the qualifications and elections of its own members; but contested elections shall be determined in such manner as shall be directed by law. And a majority of each House shall constitute a quorum to do business, but a smaller number may adjourn from day to day, and may compel the attendance of absent members in such manner and under such penalties as each House may provide.

SEC. 9. Each House may determine the rules of its own proceeding; punish members for disorderly conduct; and, with the consent of two-thirds, expel a member, but not a second time for the same offence.

SEC. 10. Each House shall keep a journal of its proceedings and publish the same. And the yeas and nays of the members of either House, on any question, shall, at the desire of any three members present, be entered on the journal.

SEC. 11. When vacancies happen in either House, the Governor, or the person exercising the power of Governor, shall issue writs of election to fill such vacancy.

SEC. 12. Senators and Representatives shall, in all cases, except treason, felony, or breach of the peace, be privileged from arrest during the session of the Legislature, and in going to and returning from the same.

SEC. 13. The doors of each House shall be open, except the Legislature have a treaty under consideration.

SEC. 14. Neither House shall, without the consent of the other, adjourn for more than three days.

SEC. 15. Bills may originate in either House, and amended, altered or rejected by the other; but no bill shall have the force of a law until it be read in each House two several days, and free discussion allowed thereon, unless two-thirds of the House in which the same shall be pending may deem it expedient to dispense with this rule. And every bill having passed both Houses, shall be signed by the Speaker and President of their respective bodies.

SEC. 16. All bills for raising a revenue for the support of the government of the Chickasaw Nation shall originate in the House of Representatives, but the Senate may amend or reject them as other bills.

SEC. 17. Each member of the Legislature shall receive from the public treasury a compensation for his services, which may be increased or diminished by law; but no increase of compensation shall take effect during the session at which such increase shall have been made.

SEC. 18. No Senator or Representative shall, during the term for which he shall have been elected, be appointed to any civil office of profit under this Nation, which shall have been created, or the emoluments of which shall have been increased during such term; except such offices as may be filled by elections by the people.

SEC. 19. No person, who may hereafter be a collector, or holder of public moneys, shall have a seat in either House of the Legislature, or hold any other office created under the constitution, until such person shall have accounted for, and paid into the treasury, all such sums for which he may be accountable.

SEC. 20. No money shall be drawn from the treasury but in consequence of an appropriation made by law. An accurate statement of the receipts and expenditures of public moneys shall be attached to, and published with the laws, at every regular session of the Legislature.

SEC. 21. The members of the Legislature shall receive, for their services, *three dollars per day*, until otherwise fixed by law; and be paid out of the public treasury.

SEC. 22. The House of Representatives shall have the sole power of impeachments; and all impeachments shall be tried by the Senate. When sitting for that purpose, the Senators shall be upon oath or affirmation; and no person shall be convicted without the concurrence of two-thirds of the members present. Judgment in cases of impeachment shall not extend only to removal from office, and disqualification from holding any office of honor, trust, or profit, under this Nation; but the parties convicted shall, nevertheless, be subject to indictment, trial, and punishment, according to law.

SEC. 23. All officers against whom articles of impeachment may be preferred shall be suspended from the exercise of the duties of their office during the pendency of their impeachment. The appointing power shall make a provisional appointment to fill the vacancy occasioned by the suspension of an officer, until the decision on the impeachment.

SEC. 24. The Legislature shall provide for the trial, punishment, and removal from office, of all other officers of this Nation, by indictment or otherwise.

ARTICLE 5.

EXECUTIVE DEPARTMENT.

SEC. 1. The Supreme Executive power of this Nation shall be vested in a Chief Magistrate, who shall be styled "The Governor of the Chickasaw Nation."

SEC. 2. The Governor shall be elected by the electors of the Nation, at the time and places of elections for members of the Legislature, and shall hold his office two years from the time of his installation, and until his successor shall be qualified; but shall not be eligible for more than four years in any term of six years.

SEC. 3. No person shall be eligible to the office of Governor unless he shall have attained the age of thirty years, and shall have been a resident of this Nation for one year next preceding his election. Neither shall any person, except a Chickasaw, by birth, or an adopted member of the tribe, at the time of the adoption of this constitution, be eligible to the office of Governor.

SEC. 4. The returns of every election for Governor shall be made out, sealed up, and transmitted to the National Secretary, at the seat of Government, who shall deliver it to the Speaker of the House of Representatives, during the first day of its organization, who shall proceed immediately to open and count the votes in the presence of both Houses of the Legislature. The person having a majority of the whole number of said votes shall be declared by the Speaker to be Governor. But if no person shall have a majority of said votes, or if two or more shall have an equal and the greatest number of said votes then said Legislature, on the second day of its organization, by joint vote of both Houses, shall proceed, without debate, to choose a Governor from a list of the names of the two persons having the greatest number of votes, or of the names of the persons having an equal and highest number of votes, so returned, as aforesaid.

SEC. 5. The Governor shall receive for his services a compensation, to be fixed by law, which shall neither be increased nor diminished during his continuance in office. The first Governor shall receive an annual salary of *seven hundred and fifty dollars*, and no more.

SEC. 6. He shall take care that the laws be faithfully executed.

SEC. 7. He may, by proclamation, on extraordinary occasions, convene the Legislature; and shall state to both Houses, when assembled, the purpose for which they shall have been convened. He shall, from time to time, give to the Legislature information, in writing, of the state of the Government; and recommend to their consideration such measures as he may deem expedient.

SEC. 8. In case of a disagreement between the two Houses with respect to the time of adjournment, the Governor shall have the power to adjourn the Legislature to such time as he may think proper: *Provided*, it be not beyond the time fixed for the meeting of the next Legislature.

SEC. 9. No person shall, while holding any office under this Nation, exercise the office of Governor.

SEC. 10. There shall be a seal of this Nation, which shall be kept by the Governor, and used by him officially; and shall be called "The Great Seal of the Chickasaw Nation."

SEC. 11. All commissions shall be in the name and by authority of the Chickasaw Nation, and be sealed with the Great Seal, signed by the Governor, and attested by the National Secretary.

SEC. 12. Every bill which shall have passed both Houses of the Legislature, shall be presented to the Governor; if he approve, he shall sign it; but if not, he shall return it to the House in which it shall have originated, who shall enter the objections at large upon the Journal, and proceed to reconsider it. If, after such reconsideration, two-thirds of the members present shall agree to pass the bill, it shall be sent, with the objections, to the other House, by which it shall likewise be reconsidered. If approved by two-thirds of the members present of that House, it shall become a law. But in each case, the votes of both Houses shall be determined by yeas and nays. And the names of the members voting for and against the bill, shall be entered on the Journals of each House respectively. If any bill shall not be returned by the Governor within three days (Sundays excepted,) after it shall have been presented to him, the same shall be a law, in like manner as if he had signed it. Every bill presented to the Governor one day previous to the adjournment of the Legislature, and not returned to the House in which it originated, before its adjournment, shall become a law, and have the same force and effect as if signed by the Governor.

SEC. 13. Every order, resolution, or vote, to which the concurrence of both Houses of the Legislature may be necessary, except on questions of adjournment, shall be presented to the Governor, and before it shall take effect be approved by him; or being disapproved, shall be re-passed by both Houses, according to the rules and limitations prescribed in the case of a bill.

SEC. 14. Whenever the office of Governor shall become vacant by death, resignation, removal from office, or otherwise, the President of the Senate shall exercise the office of Governor until another Governor shall be duly qualified; and in case of the death, resignation, removal from office, or other disqualification of the President of the Senate, so exercising the office of Governor, the Speaker of the House of Representatives shall exercise the office until the President of the Senate shall have been chosen. And when the office of Governor, President of the Senate, and Speaker of the House, shall become vacant, in the recess of the Senate, the person acting as National Secretary for the time being shall, by proclamation, convene the Senate, that a President may be chosen to exercise the office of Governor. When either the President or Speaker of the House of Representatives shall so exercise the duties of said office, he shall receive the compensation of Governor only; and his duties as President, or Speaker shall be suspended; and the Senate or House of Representatives, as the case may be, shall fill the vacancy until his duties as Governor shall cease.

SEC. 15. There shall be a National Secretary, who shall be appointed by the Governor, by and with the advice and consent of the Senate, and shall continue in office during the term of service of the Governor elect. He shall keep a fair register of all official acts and proceedings of the Governor, and shall, when required, lay the same, and all papers, minutes and vouchers relative thereto, before the Legislature, or either House thereof; and shall perform such other duties as may be required of him by law.

SEC. 16. A National Treasurer, and Auditor of Public

Accounts, shall be biennially elected by the joint ballot of both Houses of the Legislature; and in case of vacancy in either of said offices during the recess of the Legislature, such vacancy shall be filled by the Governor, which appointment shall continue until the close of the next session of the Legislature thereof.

SEC. 17. When any office shall, from any cause, become vacant, and no mode is provided by the constitution and laws for filling such vacancy, the Governor shall have power to fill such vacancy by granting a commission, which shall expire at the end of the next session of the Legislature, or at the next election by the people.

SEC. 18. The offices of Governor, National Secretary, Treasurer, Auditor of Public Accounts, and Attorney General, shall be kept at the seat of Government; and the Governor, National Secretary, Treasurer, Auditor of Public Accounts, and Attorney General, shall attend at the seat of Government, quarterly, and during each session of the Legislature, to attend to the duties of their respective offices.

ARTICLE 6.

JUDICIAL DEPARTMENT.

SEC. 1. The Judicial powers of this Nation shall be vested in one Supreme Court, in District Courts, and in such County Courts as the Legislature may, from time to time, ordain and establish, and as may be deemed necessary and be directed by law.

SEC. 2. The Supreme Court shall consist of a Chief Justice and two Associates, any two of whom shall form a quorum.

SEC. 3. The Supreme Court shall have appellate jurisdiction only, which shall be co-extensive with the limits of the Nation, under such restrictions and regulations, not repugnant to this constitution, as may, from time to time, be prescribed by law: *Provided*, nothing in this article shall be so construed as to prevent the Legislature from giving the Supreme Court original jurisdiction in capital cases, where the Judge of the District Court may be interested or prejudiced.

SEC. 4. The Supreme Court shall have power to issue such writs as shall be necessary to enforce its own jurisdiction; and also compel a Judge of the District Court to proceed to trial and judgment in a cause; and shall hold its session twice in each and every year at the seat of Government, commencing on the first Mondays of the months of April and October.

SEC. 5. The Supreme Court shall appoint its own clerk, who shall hold his office for four years, and be subject to removal by the said court for neglect of duty, misdemeanor in office, and such other causes as may be prescribed by law.

SEC. 6. The Legislature shall, by joint vote of both Houses, elect the Judges of the Supreme and Circuit Courts, a majority of the whole number in joint vote being necessary to a choice. The Judges of the Supreme Court and Circuit Court shall be at least thirty years of age. They shall hold their offices during the term of four years from the date of their commission.

SEC. 7. The Circuit Courts shall have original jurisdiction over all criminal cases which shall not be otherwise provided for by law, and exclusive original jurisdiction of all crimes amounting to felony, and original jurisdiction of all civil cases which shall not be cognizable before County Judges, until otherwise directed by the Legislature; and original jurisdiction in all matters of controversy where the sum or amount in dispute is over fifty dollars. It shall hold its term in such place in each county as may be by law directed.

SEC. 8. Each county of this Nation shall constitute one judicial district until otherwise provided for by law.

SEC. 9. The Circuit Courts shall have power to issue all writs necessary to enforce their own jurisdiction, and have a superintending control and jurisdiction over County Courts, and of all cases of divorce, and of all suits, complaints and pleas whatever, without regard to any distinction between law and equity.

Sec. 10. There shall be a clerk of the District Courts for each county, who shall have their appointment from the District Judge, and shall hold his office for two years.

Sec. 11. The Judges of the Supreme Court and District Courts shall receive such compensation for their services as may be provided for by law; and such salaries shall not be increased or diminished during their continuance in office.

Sec. 12. There shall be established in each county in this Nation a Court, to be called the County Court, which shall have jurisdiction in all matters in controversy in any sum not exceeding the value of fifty dollars.

Sec. 13. There shall be elected, by the qualified electors of the respective counties, a Judge of the County Court, to be commissioned by the Governor, and hold his office for the term of two years, and until his successor is elected and qualified. He shall, in addition to the duties that may be required of him by law, as a presiding Judge of the County Court, be a Judge of Probate Court, and have such jurisdiction in matters relative to the estate of deceased persons; to appoint guardians, granting letters testamentary and of administration; to settle the accounts of executors and administrators, and guardians; and the District Court shall have original and appellate jurisdiction, and general control over the said County Court, under such regulations as may be prescribed by law.

Sec. 14. In the trial of all causes in equity in the District Court, the plaintiff or defendant shall, upon application made in open court, have the right of trial by jury, to be governed by the rules and regulations prescribed in trials at law.

Sec. 15. No Judge shall sit in any case wherein he may be interested, or where either of the parties may be connected with him by affinity or consanguity within such degrees as may be prescribed by law, or where he shall have been of counsel in the cause. When the Supreme Court, or any two of its members, shall be thus disqualified to hear and determine any cause or causes in said court, by reason of the equal division of opinion of said Judges, the same shall be certified to the Governor of the Nation, who shall immediately commission the requisite number of persons, learned in the law, for the trial and determination of said case or cases. When the Judges of the District Court are thus disqualified, the parties in controversy may, by consent, appoint a proper person to try the case ; but in case of disagreement to appoint a proper person by the parties, the same shall be certified to the Governor, to be proceeded with as in the case of Supreme Judges. The disqualifications of Judges of County Courts shall be remedied as may hereafter be by law prescribed.

SEC. 16. There shall be one District Attorney elected, by the qualified electors of this Nation, who shall hold his office for two years, and his duties, salary and perquisites shall be prescribed by law. He shall also act as Attorney General for the Nation.

SEC. 17. There shall be elected, by the qualified electors of each county, one sheriff, and a sufficient number of constables, who shall hold their offices for two years ; and the duties, salaries and perquisites shall be prescribed by law. The sheriff shall not be eligible more than four years in every six.

SEC. 18. All Judges of the several courts of this Nation shall, by virtue of their offices, be conservators of the peace throughout the Nation. The style of all writs and process, shall be, "The Chickasaw Nation." All prosecutions shall be carried on "in the name, and by the authority of the Chickasaw Nation," and conclude "against the peace and dignity of the Nation."

GENERAL PROVISIONS.

SECTION 1. Members of the Legislature, and all officers, shall take the following oath, or affirmation, before they enter upon the duties of their offices: "I (A. B.) do solemnly swear, (or affirm,) that I will faithfully and impartially discharge and perform all the duties incumbent on me, as ——, according to the best of my skill and ability, agreeably to the constitution and laws of the Chickasaw Nation, so help me God."

SEC. 2. Treason against this Nation shall consist only in levying war against it, or in adhering to its enemies, giving them aid and comfort. And no person shall be convicted of treason unless on the testimony of two witnesses to the same overt act, or his own confession in open court. And any person guilty of treason shall suffer death.

SEC. 3. All property, both real and personal, of the wife, owned and claimed by her before marriage, and that acquired afterwards, by gift, devise, or descent, shall be her separate property. And laws shall be passed more clearly defining the rights of the wife, in relation as well to her separate property, as that held in common with her husband. Laws shall also be passed providing for the registration of the wife's separate property.

SEC. 4. Divorces from the bonds of matrimony shall not be granted but in cases provided for by law, by suit in the District Circuit Court of this Nation.

SEC. 5. The Chickasaw captains, holding office under the Financial Constitution of the Chickasaws, shall continue to hold their offices, as superintendents of the payment of the Chickasaw annuity, until the fourth Monday in August, 1857.

SEC. 6. The Legislature, at its first session, shall determine the number of Annuity Captains, as well as to prescribe the mode and manner they shall be chosen, to superintend the payments of Chickasaw annuities.

SEC. 7. Every person shall be disqualified from holding any office or place of honor or profit, under the authority of this Nation, who shall be convicted of having given or offered any bribe to procure his election or appointment. Laws shall be made to exclude from office and from suffrage, and provide for the mode and manner of punishing those who may hereafter be convicted of bribery, perjury, or other high crimes and misdemeanors.

Sec. 8. All persons, other than Chickasaws by birth, who have been adopted as members of the Chickasaw tribe, either by common consent, in council, at any time previous to the adoption of this constitution, or who drew land and the Chickasaw annuities under the treaties of 1832 and 1834, between the United States and the Chickasaw Nation, are hereby declared to be Chickasaws by adoption, and shall be entitled to all the rights, privileges and immunities of this Nation ; *Provided*, they are citizens of either the Choctaw or Chickasaw Nation at the time of the adoption of this constitution, and have been recognized as such under the Financial Council of the Chickasaws.

Sec. 9. Any person, other than a Chickasaw, having legally intermarried with a Chickasaw woman, shall participate in the Chickasaw annuities, but shall not be eligible to any office of trust or profit in this Nation. In like manner, a wife, other than a Chickasaw woman, having legally married a Chickasaw husband, shall participate in the annuities of the Chickasaw tribe ; *Provided*, they are residents of this Nation. This rule shall cease in cases where a husband or a wife, other than Chickasaws, die, or be separated from the bonds of matrimony. But such death or separation shall not affect the rights of the children (born during such intermarriage) to participate in all the rights, privileges, and immunities of the Chickasaws.

Sec. 10. No retrospective payments shall be made, out of the Chickasaw moneys, to any person herein adopted, or which may hereafter be adopted, under this constitution.

Sec. 11. The Legislature shall have the power, by law, to admit, or adopt any person to citizenship in this Nation, except a negro, or descendant of a negro : *Provided, however*, that such an admission, or adoption, shall not give a right, further than to settle and remain in the Nation, and to be subject to its laws.

SEC. 12. Whenever two-thirds of both branches of the Legislature deem it necessary, they may propose amendments to this constitution; and if two-thirds of both branches of the succeeding Legislature approve such amendments, they shall be engrafted to, and form a part of this constitution.

SEC. 13. The Legislature shall provide for the election of all officers necessary to carry into effect the general and specific powers of the several courts of this Nation not otherwise provided for in this constitution.

SEC. 14. All marriages which may have been either solemnized by the laws of the Choctaw Nation, or by mutual consent of parties which lived together as man and wife at least six months previous to the adoption of this constitution, are hereby declared to be legalized, to all intents and purposes. The Legislature shall, by law, prescribe the mode and manner by which such marriages may be proven and recorded.

SEC. 15. The provisions of this constitution concerning the term of residence necessary to enable persons to hold certain offices therein mentioned, shall not be held to apply to officers chosen at the first election by the people, or by the Legislature at its first session; but all Chickasaws by birth or adoption shall be eligible to any office at the first election by the people, or the Legislature at its first session, who have been actual settlers of the Chickasaw Nation one day next preceding their election.

SEC. 16. All general elections by the people, for officers under this constitution, shall be holden on the second Wednesday in the month of September, in each year. Immediately after the adjournment of this Convention, the Chief of the Chickasaw Financial Council shall appoint a sufficient number of judges and clerks in the several counties of this Nation, to cause polls to be opened in their respective places of holding County Courts, as established under the Choctaw law, on the second Wednesday in September next, (A. D. 1856,) for the purpose of voting for a Governor, District Attorney, electing Senators, Representatives, County

Judges, Sheriffs and Constables. The certificates of election of Senators, Representatives, County Judges, Sheriffs, and Constables, shall be given by the judges of the election in their respective counties. And the returns for Governor and District Attorney shall be sealed up and transmitted to the Secretary of the Financial Council, to be delivered to the Speaker of the House of Representatives on the first day of its organization, who shall open the same and count the votes in the presence of both Houses of the Legislature.

SEC. 17. That no inconvenience may arise from the political separation between the Choctaws and Chickasaws, it is hereby declared, that all the rights, privileges and immunities of citizens secured under article 5th of the treaty of June 22d, 1855, to all Choctaws who are now or hereafter may become residents within the limits of the Chickasaw Nation, are fully recognized and protected. And all the rights of property acquired by virtue of the constitution and laws of the Choctaw Nation shall remain precisely in the same situation they were before the adoption of this constitution.

SEC. 18. Full faith and credit shall be given to all the acts of the Chickasaw Financial Council so far as they are not repugnant to this constitution.

SEC. 19. The oath of office may be administered by any judge of this Nation.

SEC. 20. All rights and powers not herein granted or expressed are reserved unto the people; and any law that may be passed contrary to the provisions of this constitution shall be null and void.

PUBLIC EDUCATION.

A general diffusion of knowledge being essential to the preservation of the rights and liberties of the people, it shall be the duty of the Legislature of this Nation to make suitable provision for the support and maintenance of Public Schools.

A Superintendent of Public Instruction shall be elected by joint vote of both Houses of the Legislature, who shall keep his office at the seat of government, and shall hold his office for the term of four years from the date of his election, whose duties shall be prescribed by law, and shall receive such compensation as the Legislature may direct.

The Legislature shall encourage by all suitable means the promotion of intellectual, scientific, moral and agricultural improvement; and such other means as shall be inviolably appropriated to the support of general education throughout this Nation.

All contracts which may have been made and entered into between the Board of Trustees of Public Schools and that of the Teachers shall be binding; subject, however, to the approval or disapproval of the succeeding Legislature.

SLAVES.

Sec. 1. The Legislature of this Nation shall have no power to pass laws for the emancipation of slaves without the consent of their owners, nor without paying their owners previous to such emancipation a full equivalent in money for the slave so emancipated. They shall have the right to pass laws to prevent the owners of slaves to emancipate them, saving the rights of creditors. They shall have full power to pass laws which will oblige the owners of slaves to treat them with humanity—to provide for their necessary food and clothing—to abstain from all injuries to them, extending to life or limb: *Provided, also*, that laws be passed to prohibit the introduction into this Nation of slaves who have committed high crimes in violation of the laws of other countries.

Done in Convention, at Tishomingo City, C. N., this, the thirtieth day of August, A. D. 1856.

JACKSON KEMP, *Pres. of the Convention.*

ATTEST : GEO. D. JAMES, *Sec. of the Convention.*

A. V. BROWN, *Secretary.*

SAMPSON FOLSOM,
WM. SIMPSON,
AR CHANAH TUBY, (his + mark,)
BENJAMIN MAYTUBY,
BENJAMIN S. LOVE,
CYRUS HARRIS,
JAMES GAMBLE,
MARTIN SHECOE,
LEMUEL COLBERT,
MORGAN COLBERT, (his + mark,)
ROBERT LOVE,
G. F. M'LISH,
E ME HUT TUBBY, (his + mark,)
E LAH NOON TUBBY, (his + mark,)
JOSEPH COLBERT, (his + mark,)
IM MUN TUBBY, (his + mark,)
WINCHESTER COLBERT,
CHRISTOPHER COLUMBUS,
OWN UT UBBY, (his + mark,)
EDMUND PICKENS, (his + mark,)
A. ALEXANDER,
D. COLBERT,
HENRY MCKINNY,
Capt. JERRY, (his + mark,)
Capt. LEWIS, (his + mark,)
PESUBBY, (his + mark,)
JAMES PATTERSON,
JOEL KEMP,
Capt. NED, (his + mark,)
Capt. WILSON FRAZIER, (his + mark,)
Capt. HOYUBBY, (his + mark,)
Capt. HOTHLI CHA, (his + mark,)
Capt. J. E. ANDERSON,
Capt. EMOSHI CHA, (his + mark,)
Capt. EMAR HO TI CHA, (his + mark,)
Capt. G. W. ALLEN,
Capt. PIS UM OUN TUBBY, (his + mark,)
Capt. JOHN PARKER, (his + mark,)
Capt. E LAP AM BEE, (his + mark,)
JAMES N. M'LISH,
SAM'L COLBERT,
JOHN M. JOHNSON,
WILLIAM KEMP,
HORACE PRATT.

L A W S.

An Act defining the duties of National Secretary.

Be it enacted by the Legislature of the Chickasaw Nation, that a National Secretary shall be appointed by the Governor, by and with the advice and consent of the Senate, and shall continue in office during the term of service of the Governor elect.

Be it further enacted, that he shall keep a fair register of all the official acts of the Governor; and, when required, shall lay the same, and all minutes and other papers in relation thereto, before the Legislature, or either branch thereof.

Be it further enacted, that he shall keep his office at the seat of government, or other place where the session of the Legislature may be held. He shall, in a separate book, suitable for the purpose, keep a complete register of all the officers appointed and elected in the Nation, and commission the same when not otherwise provided for by law.

Be it further enacted, that he shall be at every session of the Legislature, for the purpose of receiving bills which have become law; and, immediately after the close thereof, shall cause all such bills and all joint resolutions of the Legislature to be bound in a volume, to be kept in the office, and the date of the session to be written or stamped thereon.

Be it further enacted, that he shall copy all laws passed at each session of the Legislature, and send to each clerk of the District Courts established in each county of this Nation, with instructions to safely keep the same for the use of the county; also furnish a copy of the laws to the clerk of the Supreme Court, and one to the District Attorney.

Be it further enacted, that, in the absence of the National Secretary, the Governor shall appoint a competent person to perform all the duties required by this act, until the return of the regular Secretary to his office. The person so appointed shall give bond and security as the regular Secretary.

Be it further enacted, that it shall be the duty of the National Secretary to furnish any person who may apply for the same, with a copy of any paper, documents or records in his office, and also to give certificates, duly authenticated, certifying to any fact or facts contained in the papers, documents, or records of his office; *provided*, the person so applying shall pay a fee of *ten cents* for every hundred words; and such fees so paid shall be retained by the Secretary as compensation for such service. But in no case shall the Secretary claim, or charge his fee, when the Nation is interested, or demands an official copy or information of all the papers or records in his office.

Be it further enacted, that when the National Secretary be duly appointed, he shall, within twenty days after receiving notice of his appointment, and before entering upon the duties of his office, give a bond, payable to the Governor of the Chickasaw Nation, or his successor in office, with at least two good and sufficient securities, to be approved by the Governor, in the sum of one thousand dollars, conditioned for the faithful performance of the duties of his office, and shall take and subscribe the oath prescribed in the constitution; which, together with the bond, shall be deposited in the office of the Attorney General, and such bond shall not be void on the first recovery, but may be sued on the same until the whole amount of damages or misdemeanor in office shall be finally disposed of.

Be it further enacted, that the salary of the National Secretary shall be four hundred dollars per annum; to be paid out of the National Treasury.

Be it further enacted, that all acts heretofore passed in conflict with this act, be and the same are hereby repealed; and that this act take effect from and after its passage.

Approved, October 29, 1857.

C. HARRIS, *Governor.*

An Act defining the duties of District Attorney.

Be it enacted by the Legislature of the Chickasaw Nation, that the District Attorney, before entering upon the duties of his office, shall give a bond, payable to the Governor and his successor in office, for the use of the Nation, in the sum of one thousand dollars, to be approved by the Circuit Judge, with not less than two securities—conditioned that he will faithfully pay over, in the manner prescribed in this act, all money which he may collect for the use of the Nation, and shall take and subscribe the oath prescribed by the constitution; which, together with the bond, shall be deposited in the office of the National Secretary; which bond shall not be void on the first recovery, but may be sued on from time to time.

Be it further enacted, that it shall be the duty of the District Attorney to attend at all terms of the Circuit Courts, and conduct all prosecutions for crimes and offences cognizable in such courts; to prosecute and defend all other actions in which the Nation may be interested, and to perform such other duties as may be prescribed by the constitution and laws of the Nation.

Be it further enacted, that when the District Attorney shall fail to attend any of the terms of the courts above specified, his salary shall be liable to such deduction as may be prescribed by law.

Be it further enacted, that the District Attorney shall report to the National Secretary, quarterly, at the close of the courts of the district, in such form as he may prescribe, the number of indictments which have been found by the grand juries in the district for the preceding quarter, specifying the offences charged therein, the number of arraignments, convictions and acquittals for each offence, the number of indictments which have been disposed of without the intervention of a petit jury, with cause and manner of such disposition; and also a summary of the judgments rendered on such convictions, specifying the offences, the nature and amount of the penalty imposed, and the amount of fines and penalties collected.

Be it further enacted, that the District Attorney shall give such directions to the Circuit Clerks and Sheriffs, in the several counties, as he may deem necessary to insure the collection of all money for which judgment may have been rendered in favor of the Nation.

Be it further enacted, that it shall be the duty of the District Attorney, whenever he collects any money for the use of the Nation, to deliver to the officer, or person paying the same, duplicate receipts therefor.

Be it further enacted, that the District Attorney shall, on or before the first of October, and on or before the first of April, in each year, file in the office of the Auditor of Public Accounts, an account, in writing, verified by his affidavit, of all money received by him, by virtue of his office, during the preceding six months, and payable by law into the National Treasury, and shall, at the same time, pay such money into the Treasury.

Be it further enacted, that the District Attorney shall also file a like account, verified in like manner, in the office of the Treasurer of the Nation, of all money received by him by virtue of his office during the preceding six months, and payable by law into the treasury of the Nation.

Be it further enacted, that the District Attorney shall not act as attorney or counsel for any party an action wherein such party is charged with a crime, misdemeanor, or breach of the penal statute, nor where the interest of such party is adverse to that of the Nation.

Be it further enacted, that no admission made by the District Attorney in any suit or action in which the Nation is a party, shall operate to prejudice the interests of the Nation.

Be it further enacted, that the District Attorney shall keep in proper books, to be procured for that purpose, at the expense of the Nation, a register of all his official acts and reports, and of all actions and demands presented or defended by him, of all proceedings had in relation thereto, and shall deliver the same over to his successor in office.

Be it further enacted, that all laws and parts of laws contrary to or in conflict with this act are hereby repealed, and that this act take effect from and after its passage.

Be it further enacted, that the District Attorney of this Nation shall receive an annual salary of three hundred dollars, to be paid out of the National Treasury.

Be it further enacted, that it shall be the duty of the District Attorney to give to the foreman of a grand jury any advice or assistance he may require in his duties.

Be it further enacted, that if the District Attorney fails to attend any of the terms of the court, the Judge may appoint a person for the time being, who shall act as District Attorney for that term, and for such services he shall receive twenty-five dollars, to be paid out of the National Treasury; *provided*, such District Attorney shall give bond and security, to be approved by the court, under such penal sum as the court may determine; and such bonds shall be liable to an action in law, as prescribed for the regular attorney.

Be it further enacted, that if the District Attorney fails to attend any of the terms of the court, he shall forfeit twenty-five dollars out of his annual salary to the Nation; but if he can show any good and lawful excuse, to the satisfaction of the Judge, for not attending, he shall not forfeit any of his salary.

Approved, October 20, 1857.

C. HARRIS, *Governor.*

An Act defining the duties of the National Treasurer, &c.

Be it enacted by the Legislature of the Chickasaw Nation, That the first and every subsequent Treasurer of the Chickasaw Nation shall, within fifteen days after he shall have received notice of his election, and before he enters upon the duties of his office, give a bond payable to the Governor of the Chickasaw Nation and his successor in office, for the use of the Nation, in the sum of fifteen thousand dollars, with not less than five good securities to be approved of by the Governor of the Chickasaw Nation, conditioned that he will faithfully execute the duties of his office, and shall take and subscribe the oath prescribed in the constitution, which, together with the bond, shall be deposited in the office of the National Secretary; which bond shall be deemed to extend to the faithful performance of the duties of his trust, and until his successor shall be duly qualified, and shall have entered upon the duties of his office.

Be it further enacted, that the Treasurer shall receive all moneys which shall from time to time be paid into the Treasury of the Nation, receipting for the same upon duplicate and triplicate receipts, which duplicate shall be deposited with the Auditor, and the triplicate given to the person depositing such moneys.

Be it further enacted, that the Treasurer shall countersign and pay all warrants drawn by the Auditor of Public Accounts on the Treasury which are authorized by law; and no moneys shall be paid out of the Treasury except on the warrant of the Auditor.

Be it further enacted, he shall keep a true account of the receipts and expenditures of the public moneys of the Treasury, and close his accounts annually, on the 30th day of September, with the proper and legal vouchers for the same.

Be it further enacted, he shall provide, at the expense of the Nation, all necessary books for the proper keeping of the accounts of the Treasury; and he shall open therein an account in the name of the Chickasaw Nation, in which he shall enter the accounts of all moneys, securities and other property in the Treasury, and which may at any time be received by him, and shall state distinctly the several sources from which the revenue is derived, and the amount received from each.

Be it further enacted, he shall also open an account in the Treasury for all appropriations made by law, so that the appropriations and applications in pursuance thereof may distinctly appear.

Be it further enacted, the Treasurer shall exhibit to the Governor, on the first Monday in October in each year, an exact statement of the condition and situation of the Treasury, and of tne balance remaining therein to the credit of the Nation, with the summary of the receipts and the payment, of the Treasury during the preceding year; and shall exhibit all books, papers and vouchers, and all other matters pertaining to his office, for the examination of the Legislature, or either branch thereof, or any committee which may be by them appointed, whenever required by them so to do.

Be it further enacted, the Treasurer shall, at the close of his term of office, deliver into the possession of his successor, the moneys, securities, and all other property of the Nation, together with the books, vouchers, papers and evidences of property in his possession, and all other matters and things which pertain to the office of National Treasurer.

Approved, October 25, 1856.

C. HARRIS, *Governor.*

An Act defining the duties of Auditor of Public Accounts.

Be it enacted by the Legislature of the Chickasaw Nation, That the first Auditor of the Chickasaw Nation, and every subsequent Auditor, shall, within fifteen days after he shall have received notice of his election, and before he enters upon the duties of his office, give a bond payable to the Governor of the Chickasaw Nation and his successors in office for the use of the Nation, in the sum of fifteen thousand dollars, with not less than five good securities, to be approved by the Governor of the Chickasaw Nation, conditioned that he will faithfully execute the duties of his office, and shall take and subscribe to the oath prescribed in the constitution, which, together with the bond, shall be deposited in the office of the National Secretary—which bond shall be deemed to extend to the faithful performance of the duties of his trust until his successor shall be duly qualified and shall have entered upon the duties of his office.

Be it further enacted, that it shall be the duty of the Auditor of Public Accounts to superintend the fiscal concerns of the Nation, and manage the same in the manner required by law.

Be it further enacted, he shall exhibit to the Governor, on the first Monday in October of each year, an exact and complete statement of the funds of the Nation; of its revenues and of the public expenditures during the preceding year, with an estimate of the expenditures to be defrayed from the Treasury for the ensuing year; specifying therein each object of expenditure, and distinguishing between such as are provided for by special or general appropriations and such as are to be provided for by law, and showing the means from which such expenditures are to be defrayed.

Be it further enacted, he shall keep all accounts in which the Nation is interested, and suggest plans for the improvement and management of the public revenue.

Be it further enacted, he shall draw warrants on the Treasurer for the payment of all moneys directed by law to be paid out of the Treasury; and no warrant shall be drawn unless authorized by law, and every warrant shall refer to the law under which it is drawn; and no warrant shall be issued in favor of any person, or the agent or assignee of any person, indebted to the Nation, unless such debt be paid.

Be it further enacted, he shall preserve the books, records, papers, and other things, belonging to his office, and deliver the same without injury or damage to his successor.

Be it further enacted, he shall number each and every warrant he may draw upon the Treasurer of the Nation. The numbers shall begin with one, at the commencement of each fiscal year, and proceed, progressing to the end thereof. They shall specify on what particular account they are drawn.

Be it further enacted, he shall furnish the Treasurer of the Nation, at the end of every quarter, with a report specifying the warrants that have been drawn during each quarter; their number, their several amounts, and the names of the persons to whom payable.

Be it further enacted, the accounts of the Auditor shall be annually closed on the last day of September; and he shall exhibit all books, papers, vouchers, and all other matters pertaining to his office, for the examination of either branch of the Legislature, or any committee which may be by them appointed, whenever required by them so to do.

Be it further enacted, that the Auditor shall examine the disbursements of the Treasurer at the end of each quarter, and shall, together with the Treasurer, cancel the warrants which have been paid in such manner as to prevent their future circulation; and shall examine if the receipts acknowledged by the Treasurer during the quarter corresponded with the deposits, and if the balance of money reported to be in his possession is actually in his hands.

Be it further enacted, that the salary of the Auditor of Public Accounts shall be three hundred dollars a year.

Approved, October 31, 1856.

C. HARRIS, *Governor.*

An Act defining the duties of Sheriff.

Be it enacted by the Legislature of the Chickasaw Nation, There shall be elected by the qualified electors in each county in this Nation, one Sheriff, who shall hold his office for two years, and until his successor shall be elected and qualified.

Be it further enacted, that every person who may be elected to the office of Sheriff, shall, before entering upon the duties of his office, give bond, with two or more good and sufficient securities, to be approved by the County Judge of his county, in a sum not less than five hundred nor more than one thousand dollars, payable to the Governor and his successor in office, conditioned that he will account for and pay over to the persons authorized to receive the same, all fines, forfeitures and penalties that he may collect for the use of the Nation; and that he will well and truly execute and make due returns of all process to him lawfully directed, and deliver over all sums of money or property, collected by him by virtue of such process, to the persons entitled to the same, or their lawful attorney; and that he will faithfully perform all such duties as may be required of him by law. And shall also take and subscribe the oath of office prescribed in the constitution, which shall be endorsed on his bond, together with the certificate of the officer administering the same; which bond and oath shall be recorded in the office of the Clerk of the County Court, and then be deposited in the office of the National Secretary. Said bond shall not be void on the first recovery, but may be sued on from time to time, in the name of any person injured, until the whole amount thereof is recovered.

Be it further enacted, that whenever any person elected Sheriff shall neglect or refuse to give bond and take the oath of office, as required by this act, within twenty days after notice of his election, the office shall be deemed vacant, and the County Judge shall certify the fact to the Governor, who shall make an appointment to fill such vacancy, and after he shall qualify, as directed in this act, he shall discharge the duties of Sheriff for the unexpired term of his predecessor.

Be it further enacted, that each Sheriff shall be a conservator of the peace in his county, and shall arrest all offenders against the laws of the Nation, in his view or hearing, and take them before the proper court for examination or trial. He shall quell all assaults and batteries, affrays and unlawful assemblies ; he shall apprehend and commit to jail all felons, and other offenders, until an examination or trial can be had.

Be it further enacted, that each sheriff shall execute all writs and process directed to him by legal authoritys, and make return thereof to the proper court on or before the day to which the same is returnable. And any sheriff who shall fail so to do, or who shall make a false return on any writ or process, shall for every such offence be fined in any sum not exceeding fifty dollars, at the discretion of the court having jurisdiction, which fine shall go to the National Treasury; and such sheriff shall also be liable to the party injured for all damages he may sustain.

Be it further enacted, that when a sheriff shall meet with resistance in the execution of any legal process he shall call to his aid the power of the county. And any person who shall neglect or refuse to aid and assist any sheriff in the execution of any legal process when summoned so to do, shall be fined in a sum not exceeding ten dollars, to be recovered by proof of such neglect or refusal before the court from which such process issued, three days' notice of such motion being given to the accused party ; and the fine so collected, one half thereof shall go to the sheriff and the other half shall go into the national treasury for public purposes.

Be it further enacted, that each sheriff shall attend upon all the District and Probate Courts for his county, and in the county where the Supreme Court shall hold its session the sheriff of such county shall attend upon the Supreme Court.

Be it further enacted, that every sheriff who shall be guilty of any wilful neglect of duty, corruption, or partiality, or other misdemeanors in office,may be prosecuted before the District Court of his county, and on conviction shall be removed from office.

Approved, November 7, 1856.

C. HARRIS, *Governor.*

An Act defining the duties of School Superintendent.

Be it enacted by the Legislature of the Chickasaw Nation, That the School Superintendent of the Chickasaw Nation shall be inspector of schools. He shall visit each school or academy in this Nation quarterly, and carefully note the condition and prospects of each and report the same to the Legislature annually—to recommend any system, change or addition in the educational department he may think advisable. He shall give tickets of admission to persons applying for the same according to the existing contract of each school within the Nation; reserving to himself the right of judging the capacity of each applicant for receiving an education and of the moral character also, and may reject for a deficiency therein. That the School Superintendent reserve the right of investigating and reporting to the Legislature relative to the conduct of any teacher or superintendent of any school against whom any serious charges may be made. That the School Superintendent also reserve the right of acting with the superintendents of the schools or academies in cases where it is necessary to expel pupils from any of the public schools in this Nation.

Be it further enacted, that it shall be the duty of the School Superintendent to examine all applicants as neighborhood school teachers; to judge of their qualifications and receive certificates of their moral characters, and to appoint trustees for said neighborhood schools; and in all cases to guard well the interests and welfare of our public schools.

Be it further enacted, that at all times the sheriff or constable of the county in which an institution may be located shall be subject to the orders of the said School Superintendent: *Provided*, said order shall be for the good and benefit of said school.

Be it further enacted, that said School Superintendent shall keep his office at the seat of government, and shall preserve and keep in order all books and papers belonging to his office.

Be it further enacted, that said School Superintendent shall have the power to appoint a suitable person living near any of the public schools to act as trustee. The duty of said trustees shall be to attend to the local business and interest of their respective schools, and shall receive for their services, each, twenty-five dollars per annum.

Be it further enacted, that said School Superintendent shall attend the examinations of all the schools in this Nation and shall note the progress and course of study of each class in the institution in a memorandum book kept for that purpose.

Be it further enacted, that said School Superintendent shall receive for his services the sum of three hundred dollars per annum.

Approved, November 27, 1857.

C. HARRIS, *Governor.*

An Act defining the duties of the Clerk of the Supreme Court.

Be it enacted by the Legislature of the Chickasaw Nation, That there be appointed for the Supreme Court of this Nation one clerk, who shall be a citizen of this Nation, and the appointment shall be made by the Supreme Judges and shall be entered on record in the proceedings of the court. And the person so appointed shall, before he enters upon the duties of his office, take and subscribe the oath prescribed by the constitution in open court, and shall enter into bond with two good securities to be approved of by the court, payable to the Governor of this Nation and his successors in office, in the penalty of five hundred dollars, conditioned for the faithful performance of the duties of his office and correctly recording the judgments, decrees, decisions and orders of the said court, and deliver over to his successor in office all records, books and papers and whatever belongs to his said office of clerk, which bond and oath shall immediately thereafter be deposited in the office of the National Secretary, and shall not be void on the first recovery, but may be put in suit and prosecuted by the party injured until the amount thereof is recovered, and shall be deemed to extend to the faithful discharge of the duties of his office.

Be it further enacted, that the clerk of the Supreme Court shall hold his office for the term of four years from his appointment, but may be removed therefrom, for neglect of duty or misdemeanor in office, by the Supreme Court; on motion of which, the clerk against whom the complaint is made shall have ten days' previous notice, specifying the particular charges of negligence or misdemeanor in office preferred. And in every such case the court shall determine both the law and the facts, and whenever the necessity occurs, the Supreme Court may appoint a clerk *pro tem.*

Be it further enacted, that if any clerk of the Supreme Court shall knowingly make any false entry or change any record in his keeping belonging to his office, every such clerk so offending shall be liable to prosecution in the Circuit Court, and shall on conviction thereof be fined in any sum not exceeding one thousand dollars, at the discretion of the court.

Be it further enacted, that the clerk of the Supreme Court shall file and carefully preserve the transcripts of all records certified to said court and all papers relative thereto, and shall docket all causes brought to the court, putting all those from each county together upon the docket in the order in which he shall receive them.

Be it further enacted, that the said clerk shall faithfully record the proceedings and decisions of said court, and certify their judgments to the courts from which the causes were brought.

Be it further enacted that the clerk of the Supreme Court shall receive for his services two hundred and fifty dollars per annum, to be paid out of the national treasury.

Approved October 15, 1857.

C. HARRIS, *Governor.*

An Act defining the duties of District Judge.

Be it enacted by the Legislature of the Chickasaw Nation, That there shall be elected, by the joint vote of both Houses of the Legislature, one Judge, to be called the Circuit Judge, whose jurisdiction shall be co-extensive with the Chickasaw Nation, and shall hold court in each county of the Nation quarterly, at the court ground or such other place as may be designated by law, at such times and in such manner as may be prescribed.

Be it further enacted, that the District Judge shall organize and commence holding his court, on the first Monday in December next, at the court ground in Panola county; second Monday, in Pickens county; third Monday, in Tishomingo county; fourth Monday, in Pontotoc county, in the aforesaid month, at their respective places of holding elections, until otherwise provided for.

Be it further enacted, that the months of December, March, June and September shall be the months that the District Judge shall commence his circuit, and the Judge shall commence his circuit or open his court at the court ground in Panola county on the first Monday, at *nine* o'clock, in each of the above named months; and also open his courts in the other counties of the Nation on the days of the aforesaid months as above expressed.

Be it further enacted, that the District Judge shall hold his office for the term of four years from the date of his commission, unless he become disqualified or be removed from office for some misdemeanor or other high crime.

Be it further enacted, that the Judge of the District Court shall, by virtue of his office, be a conservator of the peace throughout the Nation. And the District Courts shall have original jurisdiction of all criminal cases, of all suits in behalf of the Nation to recover penalties and forfeitures, and of all suits against the Nation which are or may be allowed by law; and shall have power to hear and determine all prosecutions in the name of the Nation, by indictment, information, or presentment, for treason, murder or other felonious crimes and misdemeanors committed within their respective jurisdictions, except such as may be exclusively cognizable before County Judges or other courts of the Nation; and in all criminal cases have and exercise all the powers incident and belonging to courts of general jurisdiction, and of all cases of divorce, and of all suits, complaints and pleas whatever, without regard to any distinction whatever between law and equity when the matter in controversy shall be valued more than fifty dollars; and generally to do and perform all other acts pertaining to courts of general jurisdiction.

Be it further enacted, that when the Judge of the District or Circuit Court becomes disqualified from sitting upon and determining any case or cases wherein he may be interested, or where either of the parties may be connected with him by affinity or consanguinity in the third degree, or where he shall have been of counsel in the cause, the parties in controversy may, by common consent, appoint a proper person to try the case or cases; but in case of disagreement to appoint a proper person by the parties, the same shall be certified to the Governor by the clerk of the District Court of the county where the said case may be pending: then the Governor shall appoint a proper person learned in the law to try the aforesaid case.

Be it further enacted, that the Judge of the District Court shall receive for his services the sum of four hundred dollars per annum, to be paid out of the National Treasury.

Be it further enacted, that the District Court shall have and exercise appellate jurisdiction and general control over such inferior tribunals as have been or may be established in each county; and also for appointing guardians, granting letters testamentary and of administration for settling the accounts of executors, administrators and guardians, and for the transaction of business appertaining to estates; and original jurisdiction in probate matters, only in cases where the Judge of Probate is interested.

Be it further enacted, that the Judge of the District Court

shall have authority, either in vacation or term time, to grant on petition therefor, writs of injunction, sequestration, error, and all other remedial writs known to the law, returnable according to law: *Provided*, that no writ shall be granted without good cause shown.

Be it further enacted, that the said court shall have power to hear and determine all motions (three days' notice being given to the adverse party) against a sheriff, constable, or other officer, for money received under execution or other process, or order of court, which shall not have been paid to the party entitled to the same on demand, or for other defalcations of duty; and give judgment and order executions according to the laws in such cases made and provided for.

Be it further enacted, that the District Court shall have power to impose a fine, not less than five nor exceeding fifty dollars, and may, in their discretion, imprison any person for contempt of court, not less than one nor exceeding ten days.

Be it further enacted, that the District Judge, when appropriate relief is prayed for, may grant all such orders, writs or process, necessary to obtain such relief; and may also so frame the judgment of the court as to afford all the relief which may be required by the nature of the case, and which is granted by courts of law and equity.

Be it further enacted, that the Judge shall set apart a particular day, not earlier than the second day of each term, for the trial of criminal cases.

Be it further enacted, that the District Court may order a change of *venue* for the trial of any suit, civil or criminal, under the rules and regulations prescribed by law.

Be it further enacted, that it shall be the duty of the Judge of the Circuit Court to cause the judgments, sentences, and decrees of the court, to be carried into execution agreeably to law.

Be it further enacted, that when any mistake may occur in the record of any Judge, the said Judge may, in open court, amend such judgment or decree according to the truth and justice of the case; but in all cases the opposite party shall have notice of the application for such amendment.

Approved, October 17, 1857.

C. HARRIS, *Governor.*

An Act defining the duties of Clerks of the Circuit Court.

Be it enacted by the Legislature of the Chickasaw Nation, That the District Judge shall appoint a clerk for each county, who shall hold their offices for the term of two years, and shall be subject to removal, for any disqualification or misdemeanor in office, by the District Judge.

Be it further enacted, that the clerks of the District Court shall give bond, with security to be approved of by the County Court, payable to the Governor and his successors in office, in the sum of five hundred dollars, for the safe keeping of the records, and the faithful discharge of the duties of their offices; and shall also take and subscribe the oath of office required by the constitution, which shall be endorsed on his bond, and the bond and affidavit so taken and approved shall be filed and recorded in the office of the clerk of the County Court, a certified copy of which bond may be put in suit, in the name of the Governor, for the use of the party or parties injured, and shall not become void on the recovery of part of the penalty thereof, but shall be deemed to extend to the faithful discharge of his or their duties in office, and may be sued on from time to time by the party or parties injured until the whole amount of the penalty is recovered.

Be it further enacted, that the clerks shall have the custody of all minutes, records, books, and papers, that may be deposited, or that may hereafter be deposited in their respective offices; and it shall be their duty carefully to attend to the arrangement and preservation of the same.

Be it further enacted, that it shall be the duty of the clerks of the Circuit Court to keep a fair record of all the acts done, and proceedings had, in their respective courts; to enter all judgments of the court, under the direction of the Judge; and also of executions issued, and returns thereon made, in the record books furnished for that purpose.

Be it further enacted, that the clerks of the Circuit Court, at the expiration of each term, shall make out a statement of all fines imposed, penalties and forfeitures incurred, and judgments rendered at such court in behalf of the Nation, and report the same to the Judge and District Attorney.

Be it further enacted, that the clerk of the District Court in each county shall also act and perform the various duties of the clerk of the County and Probate Court which may be required by law, until otherwise ordered and provided for; and that he shall receive for his services the sum of two hundred dollars per annum.

An Act to amend "An Act defining the duties of Circuit Clerks." Approved October 17, 1857.

Be it enacted by the Legislature of the Chickasaw Nation, That instead of filing and recording the bond and affidavit of the clerks of the District Court "in the office of the clerk of the County Court," as prescribed in "An Act defining the duties of Circuit Clerk," shall be filed and recorded in the office of the clerk of the Supreme Court.

Approved, October 17, 1857.

C. HARRIS, *Governor.*

An Act amendatory to "An Act defining the duties of Circuit Clerks."

Be it enacted by the Legislature of the Chickasaw Nation, That, from and after the passage of this act, the clerk of the District Court of each county shall act as clerk of the County and Probate Court, and the bond and oath given as clerk of the District Court shall be deemed to extend to the faithful performance of the duties incumbent upon him as clerk of the County and Probate Court.

Be it further enacted, that the clerk of the District Court in each county shall keep a book for the record of all wills, deeds of gift, bills of sale and contracts, and also for the record of all important papers pertaining to probate matters. They shall also keep a book for the record of all business relating to or appertaining to County Courts.

Be it further enacted, that said clerks shall have custody of all minutes, records, books and papers belonging or appertaining to the County and Probate Courts that have heretofore existed in their respective counties, and it shall be their duty to attend to the arrangement and preservation of the same.

Be it further enacted, that for any wilful neglect of duty, or misdemeanor in their respective duties, as clerks of the County and Probate Court, they shall be expelled, as laid down in "An Act defining the duties of District Clerks," and shall be prosecuted upon their bonds.

Be it further enacted, that it shall be the duty of the clerk of the District Court to attend upon the county Judges on the day of their regular courts, and to keep a record of all the proceedings of said court; he shall also keep his record books open for the inspection of any person who may wish to see them, whenever called upon to do so, during their office hours.

Be it further enacted, that it shall be their duty to record all administrators, executors and guardians' bonds, and also all their respective reports; and he shall also have his books and papers relating to probate matters ready for the inspection of the county Judge, whenever called upon to do so.

Approved, October 20, 1857.

C. HARRIS, *Governor.*

An Act in relation to Disputed Property and Bonds Forfeited.

Be it enacted by the Legislature of the Chickasaw Nation, That from and after the passage of this act, when disputes arise between citizens of this Nation respecting the rights of property, and upon complaint being filed, in writing, before the clerk of the court having jurisdiction of the same, the clerk of the court having jurisdiction in the county in which such difficulty may exist shall issue writs of attachment to the sheriff or constable to seize and to hold all such property in custody until the court can be held and the rights of property tried; *provided, however*, when the defendant or defendants can give a bond, with good and sufficient securities, in at least double the value of the property in dispute, (in writing,) for the forthcoming of such property in dispute at the ensuing court, in the presence of the sheriff or constable, and one other witness, he, she or they may be permitted to hold the property until the court shall decide the case; and when such bond is forfeited by the defendant, he, she or they shall be compelled to pay the same.

The court having jurisdiction shall issue writs of attachment for any property he, she, or they may have, or their securities may have, and such property so attached shall be sold to the highest bidder, to pay the amount the bond was given for; *provided, however*, after judgment on a bond is rendered, and an attachment issued, the officer serving the attachment shall seize upon property belonging to the principal and securities, sufficient in amount to satisfy said bond, and proceed to sell the property of the principal first; but in case of a deficiency, shall then proceed to sell that of the security, until the bond is satisfied; and in all cases where property is held in custody for trial, or attached and sold, the party losing the suit shall pay the cost, as may be determined by law.

Be it further enacted, that the plaintiff, his agent or attorney, upon the issuing of any attachment, shall make affidavit that the defendant is unlawfully detaining his or her property, and he or she shall also swear that the attachment is not sued out for the purpose of injuring the defendant; and shall also, at the time of the making of such affidavit, give bond, with two or more good and sufficient securities, payable to the defendant, in at least double the amount of the value of the property sworn to be unlawfully detained, conditioned that the plaintiff will prosecute his suit to effect, and pay such damages as shall be adjudged against him for wrongfnlly suing out said attachment.

Be it further enacted, that the bond aforesaid shall not be void for want of form provided it contains all essential matters, and may be put in suit and made collectable in the courts in which the case was tried.

Be it further enacted, that every attachment without affidavit and bond taken as aforesaid shall be abated on motion of the defendant.

Be it further enacted, that no judgment shall be rendered in suits by attachment unless the citation or summons has been served in the ordinary mode, unless it appears that the defendant is absent from the Nation, or purposely keeps out of the way of such summons.

Be it further enacted, that the following property be exempt from execution from bonds—homestead to consist of the following property, to wit: all the household and kitchen furniture and farming utensils, two cows and calves, one work horse, mule or yoke of oxen, all the books, two sheep, five head of hogs, and a twelve months' provision for himself and family; there shall in like manner be exempt, one set of mechanical tools, such as is usually employed by and necessary for one workman at any particular trade.

Approved, October 18, 1856.

C. HARRIS, *Governor.*

An Act authorizing the Governor to offer a Reward for Murderers.

Be it enacted by the Legislature of the Chickasaw Nation, That if any person charged with, or convicted for murder, or other capital crimes, shall break prison, escape, or flee from justice, abscond or secrete himself, in such case it shall be lawful for the Governor, if he shall judge it necessary, to offer any reward not exceeding five hundred dollars, for apprehending and delivering such person or persons into the custody of such jailor as he may direct.

Be it further enacted, that the person or persons so apprehending and delivering any such persons as aforesaid, and produce the jailor's receipt for the body of such person, duly authenticated before any Judge of this Nation, that such person or persons are entitled to the reward ; the Auditor shall issue his warrant on the Treasury of this Nation for the amount thereof.

Approved, October 29, 1856.

C. HARRIS, *Governor.*

An Act to Castrate Horses, &c.

Be it enacted by the Legislature of the Chickasaw Nation, That from and after the passage of this act, if any stud horse, jack, or jack mule is found with any person's horses, and the owner be known, he shall take him away ; and should he refuse or neglect to do so in due time, or in case the owner of such beast or beasts be unknown, he shall be taken to the nearest person who understands castrating and have him altered ; and should such horse, jack, or jack mule recover, the owner shall pay to the taker up, and the person who castrated him, one dollar each.

Be it further enacted, that should the owner refuse to pay such fine, the amount may be collected by the sheriff or constable, who shall have one additional dollar for his trouble ; but should the horse, jack, or jack mule die from castration, the owner will not be required to pay anything.

Be it further enacted, if any person should castrate any estrayed horse, jack, or jack mule, the taker up of such estrays shall pay for the castration of the same, and receive his money back, (out of the part that goes to the Treasury,) when sold, as prescribed by law.

Approved, October 29, 1856.

C. HARRIS, *Governor.*

An Act in relation to Wounding, Maiming, &c.

Be it enacted by the Legislature of the Chickasaw Nation, That every person who shall wilfully and maliciously cut, maim, or otherwise injure, or disable the body of another, shall, on conviction thereof, be fined in any sum not less than one dollar, nor exceeding one thousand dollars, at the discretion of the court having jurisdiction of the same.

Be it further enacted, that the fine, when collected, shall go to the person cut, maimed, or disabled.

Approved, October 31, 1856.

C. HARRIS, *Governor.*

Be it enacted by the Legislature of the Chickasaw Nation, That on conviction of any person for having wilfully and maliciously cut, maimed, or otherwise injured or disabled the body of another, the court, in addition to the power to fine, shall have power to imprison the offender or offenders, where they are not able to pay the fine, for a term of not less than three months, nor exceeding two years.

Approved, November 8, 1856.

C. HARRIS, *Governor.*

An Act in regard to Burglary.

Be it enacted by the Legislature of the Chickasaw Nation, That every person who shall, in night or day, break open and enter a dwelling-house, or any building attached thereto, or any shop, store, mill-house, or any place of deposit, and shall steal, take away therefrom, or injure any thing of value therein, or use the same without the consent of the owner, or unknown to the owner, shall, upon proof shown to the court having jurisdiction of the same, be compelled to return the same, or pay to the owner, or injured person, double the value thereof, in money or property; but in case such person shall not be able to pay for, or return the same, when convicted, shall be sentenced to receive not less than *thirty-nine* lashes on the bare back; *provided, however*, that this act shall not be so construed as to prohibit officers from the exercise and performance of their duties.

Approved, November 8, 1856.

C. HARRIS, *Governor.*

An Act for the Election of Annuity Captains.

Be it enacted by the Legislature of the Chickasaw Nation, That there shall be four captains elected on the second Wednesday in September next; that is, one in each county, at the several places of holding elections--who shall be elected in the same manner as other officers, whose duty, when elected, shall be to register all the inhabitants of his own county who are entitled to annuity. The several captains may register any Chickasaws that may be living out of the Nation, who may wish to register under him; it shall further be their duty to attend the annuity, attend the pay table, and see the annuity paid out, and receive and receipt for such of their warriors as they may see proper; for which services they shall be paid five cents for each warrior he may have in his company, he furnishing his own clerk.

Be it further enacted, that Captain Illapomby is still continued a life captain, and shall receive the same pay as other captains.

Approved, August 7, 1857.

C. HARRIS, *Governor.*

An act for raising the Salaries of Sheriffs and Constables.

Be it enacted by the Legislature of the Chickasaw Nation, That from and after the second Wednesday in September, 1857, each sheriff and constable shall receive from the Treasury of the Chickasaws the sum of three hundred dollars per annum.

4

Be it further enacted, that every sheriff or constable who shall be guilty of any wilful neglect of duty, corruption, partiality, or any other malfeasance in office, may be prosecuted by indictment before the Circuit Court of his county, and on conviction shall be removed from office and shall forfeit so much of their salaries as the court having jurisdiction of the same may think proper.

Be it further enacted, that whenever such sheriffs or constables shall be removed from office for any of the above enumerated offences, the Governor shall have power to fill such vacancies by appointment.

Be it further enacted, that all laws or parts of laws conflicting with this act are hereby repealed.

Approved, August 10, 1857.

C. HARRIS, *Governor.*

An Act regulating the Auditor and Treasurer's duties.

Be it enacted by the Legislature of the Chickasaw Nation, That the present Auditor of Public Accounts is hereby authorized to issue warrants or drafts on the Treasurer of the Chickasaw Nation, up to the third Monday in September next, for the pay of officers thereof, and the expenses of the present session of the Legislature, where there may be appropriations authorizing the same.

Be it further enacted, that the Treasurer is hereby authorized to pay all warrants or drafts that may be presented to him, where appropriations are made for the payment of the same.

Approved, August 10, 1857.

C. HARRIS, *Governor.*

An Act in relation to Estrays.

Be it enacted by the Legislature of the Chickasaw Nation, That from and after the passage of this act all stray property, the owner of which is not known, shall be taken up and posted as follows: when any person or persons shall take up any stray horse, jack, or mule, he or they shall be required to take such stray or strays before the County Judge of the county in which he may live; then it shall be the duty of the Judge to authorize two or more persons to appraise the same, and the description and value taken down in writing by the appraisers, which description and value shall be furnished the county clerk: then it shall be the duty of the county clerk to advertise the same in three or more public places in his county; and if the owner of such property do not appear within twelve months after which time, the property shall be sold to the highest bidder by the sheriff or constable of the county, by the clerk first giving fifteen days' notice of the same at the place at which the sale is to take place; and one half the proceeds shall go to the taker up upon his paying the county clerk one dollar and fifty cents, and the other half shall go to the National Treasurer for public purposes; but should the owner appear before the expiration of the twelve months and prove his or her property before any judge, he or she shall be entitled to the same by paying one dollar and fifty cents, each, to the clerk and the taker up.

Be it further enacted, that any person who may take up stray cattle shall post them in the same manner that horses are, and sold at the same place, and the proceeds be divided in like manner, except, that should the owner appear before the expiration of the twelve months and prove them before any judge, he or they shall be entitled to the same by paying fifty cents for each head to the clerk and to the taker up.

Be it further enacted, that sheep and hogs shall be posted and dealt with the same as horses and cattle, with this exception, that if the owner appear before the expiration of the twelve months and prove them before any judge, he or she shall be entitled to them by paying twenty-five cents per head to the clerk and taker up.

Be it further enacted, that when a person having strays

running in his range and fail to post them, the County Judge shall direct the sheriff or constable to take charge of such strays, and cause them to be posted and put in possession of any other person within his county.

Be it further enacted, that all strays shall run three months before taken up and posted.

Be it further enacted, that any person or persons having taken up any stray or strays, who shall abuse or disfigure in any way, shall be subject to a fine of not less than five nor exceeding ten dollars when convicted by County Court that the offender lives in. The County Judge shall cause said fine to be collected, and when collected shall go to the owner of said property disfigured or abused.

Be it further enacted, that when persons are convicted for abusing or disfiguring any stray property, the owner or owners of which are not known, said fine shall be put in the treasury for public purposes; and the County Judge shall order any sheriff or constable to take any property that the said person or persons (so disfiguring or abusing strays) may have and sell to the highest bidder, by first giving fifteen days' notice at one or more places in his county.

Approved, August 11, 1857.

C. HARRIS, *Governor.*

An Act relating to Ardent Spirits.

Be it enacted by the Legislature of the Chickasaw Nation, That all persons are hereby prohibited from introducing spirituous liquors or ardent spirits into this Nation; and any person or persons so offending shall suffer the following penalties, to wit: any person or persons for the introduction of any spirituous liquors, for the first offence shall be compelled to pay to the court having jurisdiction thereof the sum of ten dollars, and for the second offence he shall pay to the court having jurisdiction thereof the sum of forty dollars, and for all succeeding offences, he, she or they shall pay the last named amount.

Be it further enacted, that any person or persons who shall give or sell any spirituous liquor shall be indicted before any court having jurisdiction of the same; shall be compelled to pay a fine of twenty-five dollars for the first offence, and for the second offence shall be compelled to pay a fine of fifty dollars for each and every succeeding offence of a similar nature.

Be it further enacted, that the informer in the above named cases shall receive one half of the fine so collected, and the other half of said fine shall be put into the National Treasury for public purposes; but in case the offender refuse to pay the fine, any one of the sheriffs or constables shall, by order of the court, take such property as the offenders may have, and sell it to the highest bidder for cash, by first giving fifteen days' notice, and pay the said fine from the proceeds thereof; and in case the offender be not able to pay the fine, then said offender shall be liable to be imprisoned, not less than ten nor exceeding thirty days, as the court may determine.

Be it further enacted, that any person or persons who may have or bring any whiskey into this Nation, the sheriff or constable shall destroy said whiskey or spirituous liquors; and all male citizens are hereby bound to assist in destroying any whiskey or spirituous liquors in this Nation when called upon by the sheriff or constable, and said citizen shall receive one dollar for every such service out of the fines collected; but should any citizen, when called upon, refuse to assist without sufficient excuse, shall pay a fine of five dollars.

Be it further enacted, that should any person or persons refuse to have his or her whiskey or other spirituous liquors destroyed, by taking up arms; and any sheriff, constable, or citizens, in self-defence, should kill or destroy the life of the person or persons having whiskey or other spirituous liquors, he shall be protected by the laws of this Nation; but should any offender kill or destroy the life of any person or persons who are engaged in assisting to destroy the whiskey or other spirituous liquors, such shall suffer death by judgment of the court; but should the offender only destroy or injure the property or limbs of any of the sheriffs, constables or citizens, he, she, or they, shall be liable to a fine or punishment according to the crime.

Be it further enacted, that this act take effect and be in force from and after its passage.

Passed the Senate October 29, 1856.

JACKSON KEMP, *President of the Senate.*

An Act relating to Elections.

Be it enacted by the Legislature of the Chickasaw Nation, That the County Judge shall, on or before the election, select two assistant judges and two clerks, who, together with the County Judge, shall be managers of the election, and he shall administer to each of them an oath that they will well and truly conduct the election without partiality or prejudice and agreeable to law, according to the best of their skill and understanding.

Be it further enacted, that in case the County Judge should fail to attend on the day of election or refuse to act, it shall be lawful for the electors present at the precinct on that day to appoint judges and clerks to act as managers of the election, and shall be allowed to administer the oath to each other: *Provided*, that in such cases the managers shall certify in their returns that the presiding officer failed to attend or refused to act, and that the persons acting as managers were duly chosen by the electors present.

Be it further enacted, that the polls for the general election by the people shall be opened at *nine* o'clock, A. M., and be closed at *three* o'clock, P. M.; and in case there are tie votes, the election shall be immediately run over; and the poll for the second election shall close at *eight* o'clock, P. M.

Be it further enacted, that each of the clerks shall write down the name of each voter at the time of his voting, and mark under the proper column the candidate for whom he votes.

Be it further enacted, that, immediately after closing the polls, the managers of the election shall proceed to count the votes, and give certificates of election to the required number of persons having the highest number of votes, for the different offices to which they are elected.

Be it further enacted, that, immediately after the managers of the election have counted the votes, they shall certify one of the poll-books and sign the same, and seal it up and transmit it by some responsible person to the National Secretary, to be by him deposited in the archives of the Nation.

Approved, August 11, 1857.

C. HARRIS, *Governor.*

An Act for removing the Court Ground of Pickens County.

Be it enacted by the Legislature of the Chickasaw Nation, That, from and after the passage of this act, the County and Circuit Court Ground, and place of holding elections in Pickens county, is hereby removed and located at Rock Spring, on Brier Creek, one mile east of Ish fah lah mah's, and shall be called "Rock Spring Court Ground."

Approved, August 11, 1857.

C. HARRIS, *Governor.*

An Act in relation to Perjury.

Be it enacted by the Legislature of the Chickasaw Nation, That every person who shall, on oath or affirmation before any judicial or other officer authorized by law to administer an oath, wilfully and maliciously swears falsely, shall be deemed guilty of perjury, and on conviction thereof shall be fined not exceeding five hundred nor less than ten dollars, at the discretion of the court; and shall receive one hundred lashes on the bare back, well laid on by the sheriff or constable, and also be confined one year in the National jail.

Be it further enacted, that every person who shall unlawfully and corruptly cause, or procure any person to commit perjury, shall be deemed guilty of subornation of perjury, and, on conviction thereof, shall be punished in the same manner as prescribed in the preceding section for perjury.

Be it further enacted, that every person who shall bear false witness, wilfully and of purpose, to take away any person's life, and the life of any person be taken away in consequence of such false witness, he shall, on conviction as aforesaid, be punished as is prescribed for the punishment of perjury in section first of this act.

Be it further enacted, that any person committing the crime of perjury, or subornation of perjury, may be prosecuted at any time within two years after the commission of said offence, by indictment before the Circuit Court of the county in which the said offence should have been committed.

Be it further enacted, that this act take effect from and after its passage.

Approved, October 9, 1857.

C. HARRIS, *Governor.*

An Act in relation to Trespass.

Be it enacted by the Legislature of the Chickasaw Nation, That, from and after the passage of this act, no person shall intrude on the premises of another nearer than four hundred and forty-four yards, in no way whatever, without mutual agreement between the parties; *Provided, however*, that this act shall not interfere with former arrangements or agreements.

Be it further enacted, that every person who shall wilfully or maliciously violate the foregoing act, shall be deemed guilty of a misdemeanor; and upon application being made to the County Judge, by the person intruded upon, he shall order the sheriff or constable to remove the offender forthwith; the intruder forfeiting all his labor and improvements.

Be it further enacted, that this act shall not interfere with any improvements or settlements that have been, or may be made within the jurisdiction of any public place in this Nation.

Approved, October 9, 1857.

C. HARRIS, *Governor.*

An Act making Bonds and Fines collectable.

Be it enacted by the Legislature of the Chickasaw Nation, That, from and after the passage of this act, all bonds that may be forfeited, and fines and penalties imposed, shall be collected by the courts and officers having jurisdiction thereof.

Approved, October 9, 1857.

C. HARRIS, *Governor.*

An Act in relation to harboring Runaway Negroes.

Be it enacted by the Legislature of the Chickasaw Nation, That from and after the passage of this act, if any person or persons shall be found guilty of harboring or clandestinely supporting any runaway negro slave, or slaves, or negroes indentured for a term of years, or in aiding and assisting in so doing, on conviction thereof before a court of competent jurisdiction, he, she, or they, shall, for such offence, be fined not less than one hundred nor more than five hundred dollars, one half of which shall go to the informer when collected; the other half to be paid into the National Treasury for public purposes.

Be it further enacted, that it shall be the duty of the Circuit Judge to give this act in charge to the grand jury.

Be it further enacted, that if any person is convicted, as prescribed in the above act, should not be able to pay the fine, he, she or they shall be sentenced to the National jail not less than six months, nor more than one year, at the discretion of the court.

Approved, October 13, 1857.

C. HARRIS, *Governor.*

An Act in relation to Wills and Testaments.

Be it enacted by the Legislature of the Chickasaw Nation, That from and after the passage of this act, all wills, written or verbal, made by any person of this Nation, nineteen years of age and upwards, shall be valid to all intents and purposes; and, furthermore, it shall be witnessed by two unimpeachable, disinterested witnesses, over the age of sixteen years; and the said will shall be recorded within two months after the decease of the individual making the will, in the office of the county clerk of the county in which the individual resided.

Be it further enacted, that no will shall be void for the want of form, nor no construction shall be placed contrary to the words expressed in the will; and, furthermore, that the last will and testament shall revoke all former wills and testaments.

Approved, October 14, 1857.

C. HARRIS, *Governor.*

An Act to organize the Supreme Court.

Be it enacted by the Legislature of the Chickasaw Nation, That the Supreme Court of the Nation shall consist of a Chief Justice and two Associates, to be elected by the joint vote of the Legislature, any two of whom shall form a quorum.

Be it further enacted, that the Chickasaw Nation shall constitute one Supreme Court district only; and said court shall be holden twice in each year, on the first Monday in April and the first Monday in October, and shall continue in session two weeks at each sitting; *provided*, business should require so long a time. Said court shall hold its sessions at Tishomingo City, in the county of Tishomingo, commencing on the first Monday in April, 1858.

Be it further enacted, that the Supreme Court shall have appellate jurisdiction over all manner of pleas, plaints, motions, causes and controversies, both civil and criminal, which may be laid before it from the Circuit Court of the Nation, and which shall be cognizable in the Supreme Court according to the constitution and laws of the Nation. And when the judgment or decree of the court below, in civil cases, shall be reversed, the Supreme Court shall proceed to render such judgment or decree as the court below should have rendered or pronounced; except when it be necessary that some matter of fact be ascertained, or damages to be assessed, or the cause to be decreed is uncertain, in either of which cases the cause, or prosecution, as the case may be, should be remanded for a more definite decision.

Be it further enacted, that all cases decided by the Supreme Court, the judgment or decree of the Court shall be in writing, and pronounced in open court, with the reasons of the court for the same; which shall be recorded by the clerk of the court, in a book kept by him for that purpose.

Be it further enacted, that all writs and process issuing from the Supreme Court shall bear the test of the Chief Justice of said court, and be signed by the clerk thereof, and may be directed to the sheriff, or other proper officer of any county in this Nation; and shall be by such officer executed according to the commands thereof, and returned to the court from which they emanated.

Be it further enacted, that the Supreme Court shall have

power to punish any person for a contempt of said court, according to the principles and usages of law in like cases, not to exceed one hundred dollars fine, or imprisonment not exceeding thirty days.

Be it further enacted, that the Supreme Court shall have power, if necessary, to establish rules and regulations for the government of said court; also, if necessary, for the Circuit Court, not inconsistent with the constitution and laws of this Nation.

Be it further enacted, that there shall be no reversal on an appeal; nor shall the same be dismissed for want of form: *Provided*, sufficient matter or substance be contained in the record to enable the court to decide the case upon its merits. And where the court shall be of opinion that an appeal or writ of error has been taken for delay, and that there was no good, probable and sufficient cause for taking such appeal, then, and in that case, the appellant, if he be the defendant in the court below, shall pay all necessary costs that shall arise.

Be it further enacted, that the causes on the docket of said court may be tried by counties, or in such order as to the Judges of said court may seem best calculated to promote the interest and convenience of the parties or their attorneys: *Provided*, that all appeals in criminal cases shall be called for trial before the civil causes from the same county, and all causes shall be tried at the term they are docketed, unless satisfactory cause be shown for a continuance.

Approved, October 15, 1857.

C. HARRIS, *Governor*.

An Act in relation to Roads.

Be it enacted by the Legislature of the Chickasaw Nation, That from and after the passage of this act, the County Judge shall have power to summons all male citizens that are under fifty years of age, and over sixteen, to work on public roads within their county, six days in each and every year.

Be it further enacted, that the County Judges shall appoint overseers, and appoint out the portion of the road they shall work.

Be it further enacted, that if any person or persons shall refuse to work on any public road, he shall be compelled to pay a fine of fifty cents for every day that he refuses to work, unless a good lawful excuse be rendered to the County Judge, after the case be reported to the Judge of such refusal or non-attendance by the overseer. The County Judges shall cause such fines to be collected by the sheriff or constable; and all fines that are collected under this act shall be used for county purposes.

Be it further enacted, that the County Judges shall notify people when they are going to work on the road, to bring with them their axes, grubbing hoes and spades.

Be it further enacted, that when there is a petition from the citizens of the county to the Judge to have a new road cut from one public place to another, the Judge shall appoint two persons to examine and mark out the nearest and best way, and report the same to the Judge; and they shall receive one dollar a day for their services, to be paid out of the road fine.

Be it further enacted, that all licensed merchants and white men that are in this Nation shall work on the road, or pay the above fine.

Be it further enacted, that all licensed preachers and school teachers, and the Governor, be exempted from this act.

Be it further enacted, that any person owning more than two male slaves, of lawful age to work on the road, he shall be compelled, under this act, to send one.

Approved, October 15, 1857.

C. HARRIS, *Governor.*

An Act authorizing the District Attorney to collect Bonds forfeited.

Be it enacted by the Legislature of the Chickasaw Nation, That all bonds given by the officers of this Nation for the faithful performance of the duties of their respective offices, and all bonds given by individuals for their appearance at the different courts of this Nation, shall be made payable to the Governor, or his successor in office; and when forfeited shall be put in suit by the District Attorney, in the name of the Governor, for the benefit of the Nation, or the party injured.

Approved, October 15, 1857.

C. HARRIS, *Governor.*

An Act in relation to Arbitration.

Be it enacted by the Legislature of the Chickasaw Nation, That when an arbitrator or arbitrators are chosen by two or more persons to decide and settle any matter in controversy, it will be necessary for said arbitrators to take an oath, prescribed by any person authorized to administer the same, to the effect that they will settle said controversy according to law and equity. After each person in controversy shall have furnished said arbitrators with all proofs, facts and statements, or any evidence they may possess in relation to said controversy, the said statements and evidence given on oath before said arbitrators, (who are hereby authorized to swear all witnesses in the case,) and after an impartial trial of said controversy, the decision of said arbitrators shall be final and binding on the parties choosing said arbitrators, and said decision shall be recorded in the county clerk's office of the county in which the case was arbitrated.

And be it further enacted, that in case said arbitrators cannot agree in forming a decision, they shall have the right of choosing an umpire, whose decision shall be final and conclusive.

Approved, Oct. 17, 1857. C. HARRIS, *Governor.*

An Act for the removal of Supreme and District Judges.

Be it enacted by the Legislature of the Chickasaw Nation, That the Judges of the Supreme and District Courts shall be removed by the Governor, on the address of two-thirds of each House of the Legislature, for wilful neglect of duty, or other reasonable cause which shall not be sufficient ground for impeachment: *provided, however*, that the cause or causes for which such removal shall be required shall be stated at length in said address, and entered on the journals of each House; and *provided further*, that the cause or causes shall be notified to the Judge so intended to be removed, and he shall be admitted to a hearing in his own defense before any vote for such address shall pass; and in all such cases the vote shall be taken by yeas and nays, and entered on the journal of each House.

Be it further enacted, that when any of the aforesaid Judges shall be removed from office for any neglect of duty, crime, or any misdemeanor, the Legislature shall immediatelv elect some competent person to fill such vacancy.

Approved, October 16, 1857.

C. HARRIS, *Governor.*

An Act respecting Mortgaged Property.

Be it enacted by the Legislature of the Chickasaw Nation, That if any person or persons shall give a mortgage or deed of trust upon any personal or movable property, and shall remove the same from this Nation, or shall sell or otherwise dispose of the same within the limits of the Nation, with intent to defraud the mortgagee, or person for whose benefit the deed of trust was given, such person so offending shall be deemed guilty of grand larceny, and shall be punished accordingly.

Approved, October 17, 1857.

C. HARRIS, *Governor.*

An Act to organize County Courts.

Be it enacted by the Legislature of the Chickasaw Nation, That there shall be established in each county a court, to be called " County Court." which shall have jurisdiction in all matters in controversy, in any sum not exceeding the value of fifty dollars.

Be it further enacted, that there shall be elected by the qualified electors of the respective counties a Judge of the County Court, to be commissioned by the Governor, and shall hold his office for the term of two years, or until his successor is elected and qualified, (unless he be removed for some misdemeanor in office or other disqualification.)

Be it further enacted, that every County Judge shall have jurisdiction co-extensive with the county for which he may be elected. Every action cognizable before a County Judge, instituted by summons or warrant, shall be tried, first, before a County Court wherein the defendant resides, or if there be more than one defendant to a suit residing in different counties, then in the county where the defendant and plaintiff both reside, and the other parties required to attend, by summons or warrant as the case may be.

Be it further enacted, that the County Court shall be a court of inquiry, and shall have power to commit, discharge or remand to the court having jurisdistion for further trial, offenders against the peace. For the foregoing purposes, they shall have power to issue all necessary writs and process to carry the jurisdiction of said courts into effect; and they shall have power to bind to keep the peace, or for good behavior.

Be it further enacted, that the said court shall have the power to take probate of wills; to appoint guardians; to grant letters testamentary and of administration; to settle the accounts of executors, administrators and guardians; to transact all business appertaining to the estates of deceased persons, minors, idiots, lunatics, and persons *non compos mentis;* and the settlement, partition and distribution of such estates;

which powers shall be exercised in the manner prescribed by law.

Be it further enacted, that the County Judge shall hold his court on the last Monday in each and every month, for the trial of all civil and probate matters; but shall have power to open court on any day, (except Sunday,) for the examination of any criminal cases that may originate in his county, amounting to murder, treason, felony, or any other misdemeanors; and bind the offenders over in a bond for their appearance at the first term of the Circuit Court to be held after the crime has been committed: Provided, that there is sufficient evidence adduced justifying it.

Be it further enacted, that when any County Judge becomes disqualified from sitting upon any case by being connected with the parties by affinity or consanguinity, or by being interested, the parties in controversy may, by common consent, appoint a person to sit upon the case. But if the parties can not agree in appointing a person, then the same shall be certified to the District Judge, and he shall appoint a proper person to sit upon the said case or cases.

Be it further enacted, that when any County Judge or clerk shall be guilty of any wilful neglect of duty or misdemeanor in office, or other disqualification, he may be indicted by the grand jury of the county; and on conviction in the District Court, his office shall be declared vacant by the court, and he shall thereafter be incapable of holding any office in this Nation.

Be it further enacted, that when the record of any order, judgment, or decree of the County Court there should be any mistake, and there shall be any papers on file in said court whereby such record may be safely amended, the County Judge may cause the same to be amended in open court, according to the truth and justice of the case. But in all such cases, the person or persons to be affected by such amendment shall have notice of the application of such amendments.

Be it further enacted, that the County Courts shall have

like power to punish contempts as the District Court can or may have and exercise.

Be it further enacted, that, upon application of either of the parties in controversy, the County Judge may put the case off for one term, and upon application from the other party, he may put the case off one more term ; but upon the third term the case shall be tried, without both parties agree to put it off.

Be it further enacted, that the County Judge shall receive for his services two hundred dollars per annum, to be paid out of the National Treasury.

Approved, October 19, 1857.

C. HARRIS, *Governor.*

An Act to protect Citizens within their own Habitations.

Be it enacted by the Legislature of the Chickasaw Nation, That all citizens of this Nation having a house, inclosure, or yard-fence, shall be considered his home, his refuge, and his citadel ; and no person shall wilfully enter the same unless by permission.

Be it further enacted, that if any person or persons who shall wilfully enter the house, inclosure, or yard-fence of any person, and shall there abuse any person, or create any disturbance by threats or otherwise, shall be compelled to leave the place forthwith by order of the owner of the place, or his or her representative, and shall also be liable to an indictment in the County Court, and, when convicted, be made to pay a fine not less than five nor exceeding fifty dollars, at the discretion of the court having jurisdiction of the same.

Be it further enacted, that if resistance to the order be shown by the disturber of the peace, by his taking up or showing any dangerous weapons, such as gun, pistol, knife, or any kind of weapons from which a person's life may be endangered, and should the owner of the place or his representative be compelled to kill him in order to save life, he shall be protected by the laws of this Nation.

Be it further enacted, that if any person shall wilfully enter another person's house and destroy any furniture, or shall kill, destroy or injure any stock within the bounds allotted to an actual settler, shall be liable to an indictment in the court having jurisdiction of the same; and when convicted, shall, by order of the court, make a full indemnity to the person injured, and shall be fined in any sum not less than fifty nor exceeding five hundred dollars, as the court shall determine.

Be it further enacted, that the above act shall not be so construed as to prohibit any of the proper officers from the discharge and exercise of their duties.

Approved, October 20, 1857.

C. HARRIS, *Governor.*

An Act in relation to Arson.

Be it enacted by the Legislature of the Chickasaw Nation, That, from and after the passage of this act, every person who shall wilfully and maliciously burn any dwelling house, store, corn house, or any other outhouses of value, or shall aid or instigate to have it done, shall be deemed guilty of arson; and, upon conviction thereof, shall be compelled by order of the court having jurisdiction thereof to pay to the party injured a full indemnity for damages done, and shall on receive his bare back *thirty-nine* lashes.

Be it further enacted, that if the offender should not be able to pay the whole amount of damages sustained, or shall be able to pay only in part, then he shall be confined in the National jail not less than three nor more than six months, at the discretion of the court; and shall receive another *thirty-nine* lashes on his bare back.

Approved, October 21, 1857.

C. HARRIS, *Governor.*

An Act in relation to Treason and Murder.

Be it enacted by the Legislature of the Chickasaw Nation, That, from and after the passage of this act, every person owing allegiance to this Nation who shall levy war against it, or adhere to its enemies, giving them aid and support, or shall carry on any treasonable or treacherous correspondence with them, shall be deemed guilty of treason, and, upon conviction thereof by the testimony of two credible witnesses to the same overt act of which such person shall be indicted, or upon the voluntary confession of the party accused in open court, shall suffer death.

Be it further enacted, that every person who shall wilfully and maliciously kill any person within this Nation, or shall aid or abet, or instigate the killing of any person as aforesaid, shall be deemed guilty of murder in the first degree, and, on conviction thereof, shall suffer death.

Be it further enacted, that every person who shall kill another without premeditated malice shall be deemed guilty of murder in the second degree, and, on conviction thereof, shall be imprisoned not less than one nor exceeding five years in the dungeon of the National jail, at the discretion of the court.

Be it further enacted, that any person who shall kill another in defense of himself or family, shall be deemed justifiable; though in all cases of self-defense it must appear that the danger was so urgent and pressing, that in order to save his own life, or prevent his receiving great bodily injury, before the mortal blow or injury was given.

Be it further enacted, that any person who kills another, in trying to arrest the person killed, for treason or any other high crime or misdemeanor, or in discharge of any duty required by law, or by accident or misfortune, then, and in that case, the party accused shall be for the same fully acquitted and discharged.

Be it further enacted, that the mode of inflicting capital punishment shall be by hanging by the neck until dead.

Approved, Oct. 22, 1857. C. HARRIS, *Governor.*

An Act authorizing County Courts to appoint County Treasurer.

Be it enacted by the Legislature of the Chickasaw Nation, That there shall be in each county of this Nation a County Treasurer, who shall be appointed by the County Court, and shall hold his office for the term of two years from the day of his appointment, and until his successor shall have been duly appointed and qualified, unless sooner removed by the County Court, as hereinafter provided.

Be it further enacted, that any person who shall be appointed County Treasurer, shall, within twenty days after receiving notice of his appointment, and before entering upon the duties of his office, give a bond to the County Court of his county, with at least two good and sufficient securities, to be approved by the Circuit Judge of the District Court, in such sum as they may deem necessary, conditioned that such Treasurer shall faithfully execute the duties of his office, and pay over according to law all moneys which shall come into his hands as County Treasurer, and render a just and true account thereof to the said court at each and every regular term of said court. And such Treasurer shall take and subscribe the oath prescribed by the constitution, which, together with the bond, shall be deposited in the County Court of his county.

Be it further enacted, that it shall be the duty of the County Treasurer to receive all money belonging to the county, from whatever source they may be derived; and to pay and apply the same as required by law, in such manner as the County Court may require and direct.

Be it further enacted, that the County Treasurer shall keep a just and true account of the receipts and expenditures of all money which shall come into his hands by virtue of his office, and render a detailed report at every regular term of the County Court of his county; as well as of all money received and disbursed by him, and of all other proceedings in his office; and shall exhibit to said court, at every such term, all his books and accounts for their inspection;

and all vouchers relating to the same to be audited and allowed.

Be it further enacted, that he shall deliver the moneys securities, and all other property of the county in his hands, together with all documents, instruments of writing, papers and books belonging to or for the use of the county, to his successor in office, and perform all other such duties or acts as may be required of him by said County Court.

Be it further enacted, that the County Treasurer shall not pay any money out of the County Treasury except in pursuance of a certificate or warrant from the County Court of his county.

Be it further enacted, that all moneys arising from fines imposed upon persons for selling, giving, or introducing whiskey or other intoxicating liquors into this Nation, after paying the sheriff, constable or informer one half of the fine, the remaining half shall be paid into the County Treasury where such fines were imposed, for the use of the county.

Be it further enacted, that all money arising from the sale of strays, after paying the taker up one half, the residue shall be paid into the County Treasury where such strays were taken up; also all money arising from fines imposed upon persons refusing to assist the sheriff or constable to destroy whiskey, or other intoxicating liquors, after paying the informer one half, shall be paid into the County Treasury for county purposes.

Be it further enacted, that the County Court shall order the payment of one dollar out of the County Treasury, in favor of any person who may have assisted the sheriff or constable in destroying whiskey or other intoxicating liquors, in every case where such assistance had been rendered, verified by a certificate of the sheriff or constable who may have authorized the call for assistance in such an emergency.

Be it further enacted, that the County Court shall pay out of the county fund one dollar per day to every individual employed or summoned by the sheriff or constable to assist them in arresting any person for a violation of the laws of this Nation.

Be it further enacted, that the County Treasurer shall receive, and may retain in his hands, such compensation, not exceeding five per cent. upon the amount received and disbursed by him, as the County Court may, in their discretion, allow.

Be it further enacted, that all laws passed in conflict with this, be, and is hereby repealed, and that this act take effect from and after its passage.

Approved, October 22, 1856.

C. HARRIS, *Governor.*

An Act appropriating $5,500 *for the Burney Institute.*

Be it enacted by the Legislature of the Chickasaw Nation, That C. S. Love and the National School Superintendent be and they are hereby appointed a Building Committee, in conjunction with the agent of the Board, to contract for and superintend the erection of the necessary buildings for Burney Female Academy.

Be it further enacted, that the sum of five thousand five hundred dollars of the lease fund, now in the Treasury, be and the same is hereby appropriated to the erection of said buildings.

Be it further enacted, that the above appropriation shall remain in the hands of the National Treasurer to carry into effect any contract that the aforesaid committee may make for the erection of said buildings.

Be it further enacted, that the Auditor shall not issue any order for any part of said money without a certificate, signed by the whole number of the committee, that certain conditions of the contract had been complied with, or a certain amount of material had been furnished; then upon such certificate the Auditor shall issue a warrant on the Treasurer for the amount that is specified in the aforesaid certificate, and the certificate shall be a voucher for the Auditor.

Be it further enacted, that should the five thousand five hundred dollars herein appropriated not be sufficient to complete said buildings, then the committee shall have power to use so much of the annual appropriation for 1858 as may be necessary to complete them; *provided, however*, that they shall not use more than five hundred dollars out of said appropriation of 1858.

Be it further enacted, that said committee shall have the right to pull down and use all the buildings now commenced for said school, together with all the brick, lime, lumber and other materials in and about said buildings.

Approved, October 23, 1857.

C. HARRIS, *Governor.*

An Act in relation to Accessory to Murder.

Be it enacted by the Legislature of the Chickasaw Nation, That every person who shall be accessory, before the fact, to any murder, arson, or robbery, shall, on conviction thereof, be imprisoned in the National jail not less than six nor exceeding twelve months, at the discretion of the court.

Approved, October 23, 1857.

C. HARRIS, *Governor.*

An Act to suppress Gambling.

Be it enacted by the Legislature of the Chickasaw Nation, That the game of faro, roulette, monte, and all other games of chance, which are played by persons holding banks for the purpose of inviting or receiving betters thereto, within this Nation, are hereby made penal offences, and shall be punished as hereinafter provided.

Be it further enacted, that any person within this Nation who shall keep a bank for either of the above-mentioned games, or any other game of their character, or shall in any way be employed as a dealer, or assistant to any one, or either of them, shall, on conviction thereof, be deemed guilty of a misdemeanor, and shall be fined in a sum not exceeding one thousand nor less than one hundred dollars ; one half of the fine received to go to the county where the gaming was done, and the other half to the informer who shall prosecute the offender to conviction upon other evidence than his own oath.

Be it further enacted, that betting of checks, notes of hand, or any other representative of money, or articles of value, shall be construed as coming under the provisions of this act; nor shall a person charged with the above-mentioned offences be discharged for informality in an indictment.

Be it further enacted, that on the trial of any person or persons for the commission of any offence mentioned in this act, it shall be sufficient for the indictment to charge, that the person or persons so offending did play at cards, without stating what description of game was played; and upon making proof of the charge, it shall be considered that the offence is made out, without proving what the game was.

Be it further enacted, that if any person or persons shall bet, or be concerned in betting, at any gaming table, bank, or banks mentioned in the preceding chapter of this act, or at any other gambling device whatever, such person or persons so offending shall, upon conviction thereof by indictment, be fined in any sum not less than ten nor more than fifty dollars.

Be it further enacted, that if any person shall permit any game prohibited by this act to be played in his or her house, or shall rent any room for such purpose, he or she so offending shall, on conviction, be fined not less than twenty-five nor more than fifty dollars.

Be it further enacted, that it shall be the duty of every Judge of the County Court within this Nation to take cognizance of any offence against this act which shall come to his knowledge, by information or otherwise; and shall thereupon forthwith be examined, and held to bail at the next term of the District Court.

Be it further enacted, that if any person or persons other than a citizen of this Nation shall be charged with playing any of the games enumerated under this act, he or they shall be held to bail in any sum not less than twice the amount of the fine that may be imposed when convicted; nor his or their bonds received, unless the securities be citizens of this Nation.

Be it further enacted, that it shall be the duty of every sheriff, constable and other officers of the County Court, and of the grand juries of the counties of this Nation, to inquire into and present all persons guilty of a violation of the above act; and it shall be the duty of the Judge of the District Court to give it in charge to the grand jury.

Be it further enacted, that this act shall take effect from and after the date of its passage.

Be it further enacted, that in all convictions and fines imposed under this act, one half shall go to the informer, and the other half go to the county where such conviction or fines shall be imposed, for county purposes.

Approved, October 23, 1857.

C. HARRIS, *Governor.*

An Act in relation to Collection of Bonds and Fines.

Be it enacted by the Legislature of the Chickasaw Nation, That upon the forfeiture of any bond within this Nation, the judge of the court in which said bond was forfeited shall issue a writ of citation, for the principal and securities to appear at the succeeding term of the court, to show cause why final judgment should not be rendered against them for the amount of the aforesaid bond; and upon no cause being shown, the judge shall order the clerk to enter up final judgment against the principal and his securities for the amount of the aforesaid bond.

Be it further enacted, that it shall be the duty of the clerk to issue a writ of execution against the delinquents in said bond returnable in thirty days, and also renewable at the end of every thirty days.

Be it further enacted, that it shall be the duty of the sheriff or constable upon receiving an execution, to immediately levy upon a sufficient amount of property to satisfy said execution; and upon giving fifteen days' notice, in at least three public places within his county, he shall proceed to offer said property to the highest bidder, for cash, or sufficient amount of said property to satisfy the aforesaid execution.

Be it further enacted, that if property sufficient cannot be found within the Nation to satisfy a judgment within one year after said judgment has been rendered, the said judgment shall be considered satisfied in full.

Be it further enacted, that all fines shall be collected in the same manner that is prescribed for the collection of bonds in the preceding section of this act.

Approved, October 24, 1857.

C. HARRIS, *Governor.*

An Act in relation to Juries.

Be it enacted by the Legislature of the Chickasaw Nation, That the County Judge of each county be required to furnish the District Clerk with a list of all the persons that are under the age of sixty, and over the age of nineteen years, that are competent to serve as jurors.

Be it further enacted, that it shall be the duty of the clerk of the District Court to procure a book for the purpose of entering the names of the persons in, that are furnished him by the County Judge; and it shall also be the duty of the clerk to write the names of the persons furnished upon slips of paper, and put the said names into a box (or something else), and the clerk shall proceed to draw out of the box twenty-four names; and the names that are drawn out shall be nserted in the jury book; the persons drawn out of the box shall serve as jurors at the next term of the court succeeding the drawing.

Be it further enacted, that it shall be the duty of the clerk immediately after the draft has been made, to issue a notice or subpœna for each of the persons that were drawn, returnable at the next term of the District Court.

Be it further enacted, that it shall be the duty of the sheriff, or constable, to summon the jurors at least five days before court; which may be done by giving him the summons, or leaving it at his usual place of abode, with some person over the age of twelve years, notifying him to appear according to such summons.

Be it further enacted, that any juror who fails to appear according to such summons shall pay a fine not exceeding ten nor less than five dollars, unless a good cause be shown to the Judge at or before the next term of the court.

Be it further enacted, that in case the persons do not all appear, the Judge may order the sheriff or constable to summon a sufficient number of by-standers to fill the vacancies occasioned by the non-appearance of the persons summoned.

Be it further enacted, that it shall be the duty of the grand jurors to enquire into, and present to the District Attorney, all treasons, murders, felonies or other misdemeanors against the laws of this Nation, within their respective counties; and it shall require five out of the seven, to furnish an indictment against any person for violating the laws of this Nation.

Be it further enacted, that when the grand jury is sitting for that purpose, it shall have power to summon any person or persons as witnesses against offenders of the laws of this Nation; and the sheriff or constable shall be subject to its orders, to cause the attendance of such witnesses.

Be it further enacted, that all indictments shall be made out in writing, and the names of the witnesses written upon each one.

Be it further enacted, that it shall be the duty of the Judge to swear the grand jurors, and to charge them upon their duties; he shall also appoint one of the seven to act as foreman. And it shall also be the duty of the District Attorney to advert with them whenever called upon to do so.

Be it further enacted, that the remaining jurors, after the grand jury shall have been drawn, as required in this act, shall constitute the petit jury, and sit for the trial of all cases that may come before the District Court at the time for which they were summoned to attend, under the following rules and regulations, viz: The names of the petit jury shall be written down, and the clerk shall first present the list to the defendant, who shall object to one juryman, then the plaintiff to another, and so on alternately till the number is reduced to twelve persons, who shall sit for the trial and determination of the case for which they were chosen: *provided*, either or both parties may object to two additional jurymen, by assigning such reasons as the court may deem sufficient; in which case the Judge shall order the sheriff, or other officer, to summon a sufficient number of disinterested men to serve in the place of those that may be objected to.

Be it further enacted, that the concurrence of all the twelve jurors who may sit to try any case shall be necessary to a decision.

Be it further enacted, that the Judge shall have power to keep the jury out until he becomes satisfied that they can not come to a decision.

Be it further enacted, that the jury shall each receive one dollar and fifty cents per day for every day that they are detained by the court; and they shall also receive five cents per mile, going to and returning from court.

Be it further enacted, that in all civil cases the clerk shall assess the fees of the petit jury against the party that loses the case; and it shall be the duty of the Judge to render judgment against the party that loses, in favor of the petit jury.

Be it further enacted, that in all cases where the Nation is plaintiff (with the exception in cases of murder,) the party losing the case shall pay the cost of the jury; and it shall also be the duty of the clerk to assess the fees of the jury accordingly; and in all cases of murder, the Nation shall pay the whole of the costs.

Be it further enacted, that it shall be the duty of the clerk to issue to each one of the petit jury that are entitled to their pay from the Nation, and also to the grand jury, a certificate stating the amount due to each one of the jury; and it shall be the duty of the Auditor to issue a warrant to such persons named in the aforesaid certificate, for the amount called for in each certificate on the Treasurer of the Nation.

Be it further enacted, that it shall be the duty of the clerk to report to the Auditor, quarterly, the number of persons having jury tickets, and the amount called for in said tickets.

Be it further enacted, that in all cases where the defendant against the Nation loses, it shall be the duty of the clerk to assess the fees against the defendant; and it shall be the duty of the Judge to render a judgment against the person losing the case, in favor of the jurymen; and said fees shall be collected by law, according to the form laid down for the collection of bonds and fines.

Approved, October 24, 1857.

C. HARRIS, *Governor*.

An Act relating to Salt Springs and other Minerals.

Be it enacted by the Legislature of the Chickasaw Nation, That from and after the passage of this act, if any citizen of this Nation, finding or having found any salt springs, or other valuable minerals, shall be entitled to the unrestricted right of one mile square; *Provided*, *however*, that this act shall not conflict with former actual locations. And the above act shall not be so construed as to debar citizens of this Nation from the free use of the oil springs.

Approved, November 18, 1857.

C. HARRIS, *Governor.*

An Act prohibiting Negroes from holding Property.

Be it enacted by the Legislature of the Chickasaw Nation, That from forty days after the passage of this act, no negro slave in this Nation shall own any horse, mule, cow, hog, sheep, gun, pistol, or knife over four inches long in the blade.

Be it further enacted, that should any negro be caught with any property named in the above act, it shall be taken from him or them, by the proper officer or officers, and sold, by order of the court having jurisdiction, to the highest bidder for cash; one half of which shall go to the officer who collects it, and the other half shall be paid into the County Treasury for county purposes; and the negro shall receive thirty-nine lashes on the bare back, by the sheriff or constable.

Be it further enacted, that should any citizen of this Nation claim property supposed to belong to a negro, he, she, or they, shall be cited to appear before the County Judge of the proper county, and shall be compelled to testify on oath to the validity of such property. And should any person be convicted of falsely claiming any of the property named in the preceding sections, he, she, or they, so offending, shall be deemed guilty of perjury, and shall be punished accordingly.

Be it further enacted, that if any negro be caught with any spirituous liquors in this Nation, he, she, or they shall receive thirty-nine lashes on the bare back, for every such offence, by the sheriff or constable.

Approved, November 19, 1857.

C. HARRIS, *Governor.*

An Act in relation to one person threatening the life of another.

Be it enacted by the Legislature of the Chickasaw Nation, That from and after the passage of this act, if any person or persons shall make any threats against the life of another person, he or they shall be arraigned before any court having jurisdiction of the same; and if satisfactory evidence be found against him or them, it shall be the duty of said court to bind him or them over to keep the peace, in a bond not less than fifty nor exceeding three hundred dollars, in any reasonable length of time, at the discretion of the court.

Be it further enacted, that should the person or persons, after having been bound over to keep the peace, make any further threats or misbehavior, upon conviction thereof the the court shall order the sheriff or constable to collect said bond; and when collected the money shall be placed in the National Treasury for public purposes.

Be it further enacted, that if any person or persons violating the above act, and are not able to pay said bond, he or they shall be imprisoned in the National jail, not less than three nor more than six months.

Approved, November 19, 1857.

C. HARRIS, *Governor.*

An Act in relation to Abolitionism.

Be it enacted by the Legislature of the Chickasaw Nation, That, from and after the passage of this act, all white persons known to be abolitionists, or may hereafter advocate the cause of abolitionism in this Nation, shall be deemed unfriendly and dangerous to the interests of the Chickasaw people, and shall be forthwith removed from the limits of this Nation by the United States Agent or Governor of this Nation.

Approved, November 20, 1857.

C. HARRIS, *Governor.*

An Act prohibiting Negroes from Voting, &c.

Be it enacted by the Legislature of the Chickasaw Nation, That no negro, or the descendant of a negro, shall hold any office in this Nation, or be allowed a vote.

Approved, November 20, 1857.

C. HARRIS, *Governor.*

An Act in relation to Larceny and Felony.

Be it enacted by the Legislature of the Chickasaw Nation, That, from and after the passage of this act, every person who shall feloniously take, steal, and carry away any goods, chattles, money, or other article of value, under twenty dollars, or shall be accessory thereto, shall be deemed guilty of petit larceny, and, on conviction thereof, shall restore to the owner the goods, chattles, money, or other article of value so stolen, or pay the value thereof to such owner, and shall receive any number of lashes on the bare back, not exceeding *thirty-nine*, at the discretion of the court.

Be it further enacted, that every person who shall feloniously take, steal, and carry away any goods, chattles, money, or other article of value, over twenty dollars, or shall be accessory thereto, shall be deemed guilty of grand larceny, and, on conviction thereof, shall restore to the owner the goods, chattles, money, or other article of value so stolen, or pay the value thereof to the owner, and shall receive *thirty-nine* lashes on the bare back, and may be imprisoned, not exceeding one year, at the discretion of the court.

Be it further enacted, that every person who shall feloniously take or steal any horse, mare, or gelding, foal or filly, ass or mule, shall, on conviction thereof, restore the property so stolen, or shall pay the value thereof, which shall be adjudged by the jury trying such offender, and shall be fined in a sum not exceeding two hundred dollars, at the discretion of the court, and shall receive *thirty-nine* lashes on the bare back,

6

and be imprisoned, not exceeding one year, at the discretion of the court, for the first offence; and for the second offence he shall receive one hundred lashes on the bare back, and be imprisoned for a term not exceeding one year; and for the third offence he shall suffer death, by hanging by the neck until dead.

Be it further enacted, that every person who shall feloniously take or steal any neat cattle, hog, sheep or goat, shall, on conviction thereof, pay to the owner the full value of such property, which shall be adjudged by the jury trying such offender, and shall receive *thirty-nine* lashes on the bare back.

Be it further enacted, that every person who shall feloniously steal, take away, deface, utter or falsify any record, writ, process, or other proceedings in any of the courts of this Nation, or any office for records, shall, on conviction thereof, be fined in a sum not exceeding five hundred dollars, at the discretion of the court, and shall receive *fifty* lashes on the bare back.

Be it further enacted, that every person who shall steal or entice away any slave out of, or from the possession of the owner or owners of such slave, shall be deemed guilty of felony, and, on conviction thereof, shall, for the first offence, pay to the owner the full value of the property stolen, and shall receive, on his bare back, as many lashes as the court may direct, and shall be imprisoned at the discretion of the court having jurisdiction.

Be it further enacted, that for the second offence he shall suffer death.

Approved, November 20, 1857.

C. HARRIS, *Governor.*

An Act in relation to Guardians, their duty, &c.

Be it enacted by the Legislature of the Chickasaw Nation, That it shall be the duty of the County Judge to appoint guardians for orphan children that are not of age.

Be it further enacted, that the nearest relation shall have the preference; but, if there are no relations, the County Judge shall appoint a competent person to act.

Be it further enacted, that a guardian shall give a bond and security in a sum of money equal to the amount of property belonging to such minor or minors, made payable to the County Judge, that he will truly conduct and manage his or her ward's property in a businesslike manner, and it shall extend to good management of his or her wards.

Be it further enacted, that the County Judge shall appoint two disinterested persons to appraise all the property before it is turned over to the guardian, which shall be recorded in the County Clerk's office, and the guardian shall receive for his services three per cent. out of the estimate of the property that may be turned over to his or her charge.

Be it further enacted, that it shall be the duty of the guardian to keep said minor or minors at school, and said guardian shall attend and see what progress said wards are making in their studies.

Be it further enacted, that the guardian of minors shall make an annual report of the management of his or her ward's property, and the County Judge shall have it recorded in the office of the county clerk.

Be it further enacted, that guardians shall furnish their wards with good and sufficient clothing out of the proceeds of their property; and the guardian shall keep an account of said ward's expenses, and render an account of the same to the County Judge.

Be it further enacted, that a guardian shall not sell any property of a minor or minors unless said minors are actually suffering for the want of means to support them; then, in that case, the court may grant them an order to sell any property for the support of such orphan minors; and if there is any perishable property, and the guardian can satisfy the court, then he or she may sell such property.

Be it further enacted, that all minors shall be deemed competent to take charge of their property when they marry, or a male arrives at the age of nineteen years, and a female at sixteen years.

Be it further enacted, that when a guardian shall forfeit his or her bond, the court shall order the sheriff or constable to collect as much of said bond as will pay for the property as may have been destroyed, and immediately appoint some other competent person to take charge of the effects of the minor, and turn over all the property that is belonging to said minors to the person so appointed, and he shall be required to give a bond, with two good securities, in a sum equal to the amount turned over to them by the County Judge.

Be it further enacted, that if there is any negro property, the guardian shall hire out said negro or negroes to the highest bidder for one year, and take a bond, with two good securities, for the payment of such hire, and said bond shall be collected by law.

Approved, November 21, 1857.

C. HARRIS, *Governor.*

An Act to prohibit Criminals from carrying Arms.

Be it enacted by the Legislature of the Chickasaw Nation, That, from and after the passage of this act, no sheriff or constable shall suffer or permit any criminal to come before any of the courts of this Nation armed with any deadly weapon; he or they so offending shall be fined in any sum not less than ten nor more than fifty dollars for every such offence, and the fine, when collected, shall be paid into the County Treasury, for county purposes.

Approved, November 21, 1857.

C. HARRIS, *Governor.*

An Act in relation to recording Marks and Brands.

Be it enacted by the Legislature of the Chickasaw Nation, That, from and after the passage of this act, all persons owning stock within this Nation shall have an ear mark and brand, and cause the same to be recorded in the office of the county clerk, in the county where they reside.

Be it further enacted, that if any person shall neglect to have his or her mark and brand recorded within four months from the passage of this act, he or they shall pay a fine not less than five nor exceeding ten dollars.

Be it further enacted, that all fines imposed under this act shall be collected by the sheriff or constable, by order of the court having jurisdiction of the same ; and all such fines when collected shall be paid into the County Treasury, for county purposes.

Be it further enacted, that all persons having their marks and brands recorded shall pay the county clerk twenty-five cents for such service.

Approved, November 21, 1857.

C. HARRIS, *Governor.*

An Act in relation to Constables, their duties, &c.

Be it enacted by the Legislature of the Chickasaw Nation, That from and after the passage of this act no county within this Nation shall have more that two constables, whose duties and salaries shall be the same as the sheriffs'.

Be it further enacted, that the constables shall give bond with security in the same amount as sheriffs, and said constables shall be elected in the same manner as sheriff and shall hold their offices for the term of two years from the time of their election, or during good behavior.

Be it further enacted, that sheriffs and constables of this Nation shall not hold more than one office at the same time.

Be it further enacted, that Henry Colbert, constable elect in the county of Panola at the last election day, shall hold his office until the election day in 1858, or during good behavior.

Be it further enacted, that each of the counties of Pickens and Panola shall have in service two constables.

Be it further enacted, that the Governor be and he is hereby authorized to appoint one constable in Pickens county, who shall hold his office until next election day by the people, and who shall receive at the rate of three hundred dollars per year.

Be it further enacted, that it shall be the duty of the sheriffs and constables to attend the annuities, to suppress the introduction of spirituous liquor, and keep down all disorderly behavior.

Be it further enacted, that they shall receive one dollar and fifty cents per day for their expenses during the annuity.

Approved, November 21, 1857.

C. HARRIS, *Governor.*

An Act to record Marriages, &c.

Be it enacted by the Legislature of the Chickasaw Nation, That, from and after the passage of this act, all persons marrying within the limits of this Nation shall have the same recorded in the clerk's office of the County Court in the county which they may reside.

Be it further enacted, that all persons neglecting to record their marriages within one month from the time they are married shall be fined in a sum not less than five nor exceeding ten dollars, at the discretion of the court having jurisdiction of the same.

Be it further enacted, that all fines imposed under this act shall be collected by the sheriff or constable, by order of the County Court of the county in which such violation may have occurred.

Be it further enacted, that all fines collected under this act shall be paid into the County Treasury, for county purposes.

Be it further enacted, that all marriages in this Nation shall be solemnized by any Judge or ordained preacher of the Gospel; and for every couple joined together in the bonds of matrimony, the person pronouncing the ceremony shall for every such service receive the sum of one dollar from the persons joined together.

Be it further enacted, that all persons who are living together out of wedlock shall be compelled by the County Judge to be lawfully joined together in the bonds of matrimony; and any person refusing to be lawfully joined together shall be compelled to pay a fine not less than twenty-five nor exceeding fifty dollars.

Be it further enacted, that the County Judge shall cause all fines that are imposed under the above act to be collected by the sheriff or constable; and when collected, to be placed in the County Treasury, for county purposes.

Approved, November 23, 1857.

C. HARRIS, *Governor.*

An Act in relation to the pay of Members of the Legislature.

Be it enacted by the Legislature of the Chickasaw Nation, That, from and after the passage of this act, no member of the Chickasaw Legislature shall receive pay for any adjournment of a longer period than three days.

Approved, November 25, 1857.

C. HARRIS, *Governor.*

An Act repealing all the Acts of 1856 *which are not adopted.*

Be it enacted by the Legislature of the Chickasaw Nation, That, from and after the passage of this act, all the certified copies of laws that were passed in the Legislature of 1856, that are not adopted by the Legislature of 1857, are hereby repealed.

Approved, November 25, 1857.

C. HARRIS, *Governor*.

An Act in relation to Polygamy.

Be it enacted by the Legislature of the Chickasaw Nation, That, from and after the passage of this act, if any person or persons who shall take up with another woman or man, and having another spouse alive, not being legally divorced, shall be deemed guilty of polygamy, and upon conviction thereof before the District Court of this Nation shall be fined in a sum not less than twenty-five nor exceeding fifty dollars; and shall be compelled by the court to separate after paying said fine.

Be it further enacted, that all fines imposed under this act shall be collected by the sheriff or constable, by an order of the court having jurisdiction of the same, and one half when collected shall go to the Attorney General, and the other half be placed in the hands of the County Treasurer, for county purposes.

Be it further enacted, that it shall be the duty of the Circuit Judge to charge the Grand Jury in relation to this act.

Approved, November 27, 1857.

C. HARRIS, *Governor*.

An Act in relation to pulling down fences.

Be it enacted by the Legislature of the Chickasaw Nation, That, from and after the passage of this act, any person or persons who shall be convicted of the crime or misdemeanor of pulling and leaving down any person's field or farm fence shall be compelled to pay such a fine as the County Court may estimate the damages done to the owner of the farm.

Approved, November 28, 1857.

C. HARRIS, *Governor.*

General Appropriation Bill of the Second Session of the Legislature of the Chickasaw Nation.

Be it enacted by the Legislature of the Chickasaw Nation, That the following sums, set opposite to each item, be and the same is hereby appropriated out of any money in the hands of the National Treasurer, belonging to the Nation and not otherwise appropriated, for the purpose of defraying the present expenses of the Legislature, and to carry out the various appropriations heretofore made, and to meet the current expenses of the Government, &c.

To pay and carry out the contract for the erection of a Capitol of the Nation, - -	$8,000 00
To carry into effect an act passed for the erection of the Burney Institute, - - -	5,500 00
To carry out a certain contract for the maintenance of Colbert's Institute, - - -	4,000 00
To pay Thomas Birkhead for teaching Neighborhood School, at Little Spring, in Pontotoc county, - - - - - -	450 00
To pay Jackson Kemp, as Senator 19 days, - -	57 00
" William Kemp, " 20 " - -	60 00
" John E. Anderson, " 20 " - -	60 00
" Calvin S. Love, " 20 " - -	60 00
" Col. E. Pickens, " 20 " - -	60 00
" Robert Leader, " 20 " - -	60 00
Am't carried over,	$18,307 00

	Amount brought forward,			$18,307 00
To pay	Capt. W. Colbert,	" 20 "	- -	60 00
"	Charley Brown,	" 20 "	- -	60 00
"	Capt. Lewis,	" 20 "	- -	60 00
"	James Patterson,	" 19 "	- -	57 00
"	Charley Shecoe,	" 11 "	- -	33 00
"	Josiah Brown, (Sec'ry,)	20 "	- -	60 00
"	J. Gamble, Draftsman and Interpreter,		-	60 00
"	Eme-ut Tubby, Sergeant-at-Arms to the Senate,		- - - - - - - -	60 00
"	Ker-nah-ka, Sergeant-at-Arms to the Senate,		- - - - - - - -	60 00
"	Sampson Folsom, Draftsman and Interpreter,		- - - - - - - -	48 00
"	P. M. Fletcher, Draftsman,		- - -	12 00
"	T. L. Mitchell,	"	- - -	60 00
"	Lewis Newberry, as Representative 20 days,			60 00
"	Benj. M'Laughlin,	"	- - -	60 00
"	Christopher Columbus,	"	- - -	60 00
"	Duncan Ned,	"	- - -	60 00
"	Ush-ah-lah Tubby,	"	20 days,	60 00
"	Tar-hut-Ubby,	"	20 days,	60 00
"	A. M. M. Upshaw, as Representative, 20 days,			60 00
"	Doctor Allen,	"	20 "	60 00
"	Isom Keel,	"	20 "	60 00
"	E. Shar Tubby,	"	20 "	60 00
"	Reuben Kemp,	"	20 "	60 00
"	James T. Gaines,	"	20 "	60 00
"	Dougherty Colbert,	"	20 "	60 00
"	J. D. Harris,	"	13 "	39 00
"	William McClish,	"	17 "	51 00
"	Oak-i-am-bee,	"	17 "	51 00
"	Morgan Colbert,	"	16 "	48 00
"	James McCoy,	"	11 "	33 00
"	Simon B. James, as Clerk of the House of Representatives,			60 00
	Amount carried up,			$19,999 00

	Amount brought forward,	$19,999 00
To pay	Geo. D. James, as Clerk of the House of Representatives,	60 00
"	Im-illa Tubby, as Sergeant-at-Arms,	60 00
"	Joal Kemp, as Interpreter,	57 00
"	Treasury warrant, No. 3, in favor of D. Burney,	50 00
"	T. L. Mitchell, for copying four copies Constitution,	40 00
"	Sundry persons for arresting Nathan Steward,	59 00
"	A. Harlan, for Stationery,	20 13
"	Ac-koutch-an Tubby, Sheriff, for keeping Negroes,	77 50
"	G. D. James, as Member of Called Session,	18 00
"	J. M. Johnson, boarding S. Noah and L. Baptieste,	6 00
"	S. Colbert and Kanahka, guarding Noah and Baptieste,	9 00
"	Sarah Humphreys, for house rent, use of Senate,	41 50
"	P. M. Fletcher, for searching H. Long, and Laws,	57 50
"	Susan Burney and Elsa James, as witnesses in the case of Choctaw Nation vs. John Pitchlynn,	15 00
"	A "small bill" in favor of Hetty Frazier,	1 00
"	Allen Greenwood, as Light-horseman,	2 00
"	Ish-ful-ah-ma and Sillis $10 each mis-register in 1856,	20 00
"	Hoteela, for mis-register in 1850,	12 00
"	Miney Atti-ka's child, mis-register 1856,	12 50
"	James Davidson, for mis-register in 1856,	12 50
"	Immi-ash Tubby, and family, four persons	50 00
"	Ema Hambee, mis-register in 1856,	12 50
"	Own Tambee, " "	12 50
"	Minta Hambee, mis-register in 1855 and 1856,	32 50
	Amount carried over,	$20,737 13

Amount brought forward,	$20,737 13
To pay Conchee, as Light-horseman in 1853,	30 00
" Holmes Colbert, as Draftsman,	60 00
" Elah ye's daughter, mis-register in 1856,	20 00
" William, in Capt. Inortichre's company, mis-register in 1856,	12 50
" Ema Hon Tubby's daughter, mis-register in 1856,	12 50
" Charley Sheco, as District Attorney,	2 50
" S. Colbert, for keeping a negro girl under arrest,	14 70
	$20,876 83

Approved, October 24, 1857.

C. HARRIS, *Governor.*

An Act making appropriation for the expenses of the Extra Session of the Legislature.

A list of the members of the Senate from November 9th up to the 28th, 1857 :

To pay James Patterson,	as Senator for	18	days,	$54 00
" C. S. Love,	"	12	"	36 00
" Winchester Calbert,	"	12	"	36 00
" Wm. Kemp,	"	20	"	60 00
" Charley Sheco,	"	20	"	60 00
" Charley Brown,	"	20	"	60 00
" Capt. Parker,	"	20	"	60 00
" J. E. Anderson,	"	10	"	30 00
" Col. E. Pickens,	"	16	"	48 00
" Capt. Lewis,	"	6	"	18 00
" Josiah Brown, (Secretary)		20	"	60 00
" A. McCoy, Ass't Secretary,		12	"	36 00
" J. McLish, Draftsman,		11	"	33 00
			Amount carried up,	$591 00

	Amount brought forward,		$591 00
To pay	D. Frazier, Interpreter,	14 "	42 00
"	S. D. Colbert, Sergeant-at-Arms,	12 "	36 00
"	Kah-nah-kah, " "	20 "	60 00
"	Lewis Newberry, Mem. House Rep's,	20 days,	60 00
"	Reuben Kemp, " "	20 "	60 00
"	Wm. McLish, " "	20 "	60 00
"	Morgan Colbert, " "	20 "	60 00
"	James McCoy, " "	19 "	57 00
"	Benj. McLaughlin, " "	10 "	30 00
"	James T. Gaines, " "	11 "	33 00
"	Okah Yahumby, " "	19 "	57 00
"	Eshar Tubby, " "	20 "	60 00
"	A. M. M. Upshaw, " "	20 "	60 00
"	Duncan Ned, " "	15 "	45 00
"	Doctor Allen, " "	20 "	60 00
"	Tah-har Tubby, " "	17 "	51 00
"	Isom Keel, " "	20 "	60 00
"	Ah-shar-bar Tubby, " "	19 "	57 00
"	Christopher Columbus " "	19 "	57 00
"	S. B. James, Clerk, " "	20 "	60 00
"	G. D. James, do. " "	6 "	18 00
"	Muthin chee, Sergeant-at-Arms,	20 "	60 00
"	Joel Kemp, Interpreter,	12 "	36 00
"	Thomas Mitchell, Draftsman,	18 "	54 00
"	P. M. Fletcher, do	4 "	12 00
"	Joel Kemp, for registering company in	1857,	34 60
"	Capt. Ned, do do	1857,	38 45
"	Capt. Hoth-li-che, do do	1857,	42 55
"	Capt. Illapamby registering company and pension,		160 05
"	James McLish, house rent and wood,		34 00
"	James McLish, balance due as Circuit Judge,		33 20
"	A. V. Brown, as sheriff's clerk,		55 00
"	Johnson Perry, registering company,		10 00
	Amount carried forward,		$2,243 85

	Amount brought forward,	$2,243 85
To pay	Joel Kemp, balance due as Treasurer,	19 00
"	For weapons for Sheriffs and Constables,	200 00
"	Policemen service during Annuity,	132 00
"	Cun-nul.lo-chubby, mis-register in 1856,	12 50
"	Jacob Folsom, services on boundary line,	1 50
"	Isam Sheoapa, as constable,	112 50
"	Aik-ah-cho-nah, mis-register, 4 persons in 1856,	50 00
"	Roger Perry, mis-register in 1856,	12 50
"	I-ut-Tubby, mis-register, 13 persons, in 1855,	260 00
"	Samuel M'Gee and Kun-no-yo Tubby, 1856,	25 00
"	A. V. Brown, expenses, &c., hunting Long,	150 00
"	R. J. Humphreys, jury tickets consolidated,	14 00
"	Thomas Mitchell, " " "	2 10
"	Mrs. Humphreys, boarding prisoners,	1 25
"	Bob She wah-he, as deputy sheriff 6 days,	6 00
"	A. M. M. Upshaw, " constable,	1 00
"	A. Harlan, for stationery,	10 37
"	Logan Sheopa, jury tickets,	3 60
"	Oak-chan Tubby, light-horseman,	40 00
"	William Kemp, balance on Supreme Judge,	6 50
"	Committee on Public Building, and wood,	81 50
"	J. T. Daviess, for printing laws,	210 00
"	J. C. Robinson, for clothing scholars,	700 00
"	G. D. James, for registering company in 1856,	58 50
"	Nelson Frazer, as light-horseman in 1853,	18 75
"	Muthin-chee, " 1850,	18 75
"	James T. Gaines, as Judge in 1852,	20 00
"	Colbert's Institute, for clothing the scholars,	400 00
"	Bloomfield Academy, " " "	292 00
		$5,117 67

Be it enacted by the Legislature of the Chickasaw Nation, That the sum of four thousand five hundred and ninety-five dollars and fifty-seven cents be and the same is hereby appropriated, out of any money not otherwise appropriated now in the hands of the National Treasurer, for the purpose of settling the claims and accounts that are on the foregoing part of this act.

Be it further enacted, that the Auditor of Public Accounts is hereby authorized to issue his warrants on the Treasurer to the persons and for the amounts that is allotted to each name of the preceding part of this act, and the above shall be his vouchers for the above amount to the authorities of this Nation.

—

Be it enacted by the Legislature of the Chickasaw Nation, That the sum of (472 50) four hundred and seventy-two dollars and fifty cents is hereby appropriated, out of any money not otherwise appropriated now in the hands of the National Treasurer, for the purpose of covering a deficiency of an appropriation made for the purpose of paying the members of the second session of the Chickasaw Legislature.

Approved, November 28, 1857.

C. HARRIS, *Governor.*

An Act compelling Witnesses to testify in Courts and before Grand Juries.

Be it enacted by the Legislature of the Chickasaw Nation, That any person or persons who shall, after being sworn in in open court, or before the grand jury, refuse to answer the interrogatories of the court or jury, (such questions as the court may admit,) shall be fined in a sum of not less than one dollar, nor more than five hundred dollars, as the court may determine.

Be it further enacted, that where the offender is not able to pay the fine, he shall suffer such corporal fine as the court may determine, by imprisonment in the National jail, of not less than one hour, nor exceeding three months.

Be it further enacted, that where any person refuse to make oath before any court or jury, shall suffer the above penalties and imprisonment as the court may see proper to inflict, in its discretion, and having jurisdiction of the same.

Be it further enacted, that when said fines are collected by the sheriff or constable, they shall go into the County Treasury for county purposes.

Approved, March 16, 1858.

C. HARRIS, *Governor.*

An Act in relation to Cohabiting with Negroes.

Be it enacted by the Legislature of the Chickasaw Nation, That, from and after the passage of this act, all persons other than a negro is hereby prohibited from cohabiting with a negro or negroes, under the following penalties: any person violating this act shall be compelled to pay a fine of not less than twenty-five nor exceeding fifty dollars, and compelled to separate, by the court having jurisdiction; for the second offence the penalties shall be double the above amount.

Be it further enacted, that when said fine is collected, one half shall go to the informer, and the other to the County Treasurer of the county where said case is tried, for county purposes.

Be it further enacted, that any white man living in the Nation under a permit, or citizen of the United States who shall violate this act, shall be subjected to a fine at the discretion of the court having jurisdiction, and forthwith be compelled to leave the Nation, and for ever stay out of the limits of the same.

Be it further enacted, that should the person convicted of the above offence not be able to pay the fine, he or she shall be lodged in the National Jail, not less than ten days, nor more than three months.

Approved, March 16, 1858.

C. HARRIS, *Governor.*

An Act in relation to Descent of Property.

Be it enacted by the Legislature of the Chickasaw Nation, That, from and after the passage of this act, the property of all persons who die intestate, or without a will, shall descend to the legal wife, or husband, and their children.

Be it further enacted, that in case such deceased person has neither wife, nor husband, nor children, his or her grand-children (if any) shall inherit the estate.

Be it further enacted, That in case there be no grand-children, then the brother or sister shall inherit the estate, and the next in kin shall be the father and mother, or either of them.

Be it further enacted, that in case such person has neither wife nor husband, children or grand-children, brother or sister, father or mother, then the property shall descend to the half-brothers and sisters of the deceased and their legal issue.

Approved, March 17, 1858.

C. HARRIS, *Governor.*

An Act to take the Evidence of Disabled Persons.

Be it enacted by the Legislature of the Chickasaw Nation, That all witnesses who are disabled to attend court, in case he, she or they are sick, or their family, or any other disability, shall be required to give their deposition on oath before any acting Judge, and in the presence of the plaintiff and defendant or defendants, or their attorneys, by first giving the opposite party or parties at least three days' notice of the same. If the cited party should fail to appear without good and just cause shown, the evidence taken shall be legal to all intents and purposes.

Approved, March 17, 1858.

C. HARRIS, *Governor.*

An Act in relation to Slander.

Be it enacted by the Legislature of the Chickasaw Nation, That any person or persons who shall wilfully slander, traduce or attempt to injure another's character or good standing in society, shall be deemed guilty of a high misdemeanor, and upon evidence thereof shall be fined in any sum not exceeding one hundred nor less than fifty dollars, at the discretion of the court. The fines so assessed shall be collected by the sheriff or constable of the county in which the offence may be committed, and when the fine is collected, one half shall go to the person traduced, and the other half shall be paid into the County Treasury of the county where the offence may have been committed; and if the offender or offenders of this act be not able to pay the fine so assessed, the offender shall receive not less than ten nor exceeding twenty-five lashes on the bare back, at the discretion of the court having jurisdiction of the same; and for each succeeding offence of a similar nature, he, she or they shall pay the highest amount named as a fine; and if not able to pay the amount, shall receive the last named amount of lashes.

Approved, March 17, 1858.

C. HARRIS, *Governor.*

A Resolution in relation to the Funeral Expenses of Ah-thle-yo-ubby.

Be it resolved by the Legislature of the Chickasaw Nation, That the Governor is hereby authorized to contract for all the necessary funeral expenses of the convict in prison, to be executed on the 20th instant, and also for the gallows, now under contract, and all other arrangements that may be necessary in the execution, shall be paid out of the first moneys that shall come into the National Treasury; the

Auditor shall issue his warrants for the same upon the vouchers of the Governor.

Be it further resolved, that the Governor is authorized to send some person around to notify the citizens that the execution will come off at that time.

Approved, March 17, 1858.

C. HARRIS, *Governor.*

A Resolution for the selection of a Burying Ground.

Be it resolved by the Legislature of the Chickasaw Nation, That the Governor be and he is hereby requested to appoint two persons to select a burying ground (to be kept sacred), for the burying of all culprits of the Chickasaw Nation who may be executed.

Approved, March 17, 1858.

C. HARRIS, *Governor.*

An Act to fine Persons who are found with Whiskey in Possession.

Be it enacted by the Legislature of the Chickasaw Nation, That when any person or persons are found with whiskey, or other spirituous liquors, in this Nation, and it can not be proven that the possessor or holder introduced, or is selling, or has been selling or bartering it, the person so found with whiskey, or other spirituous liquors, in their possession, shall be compelled to pay a fine of from five to fifteen dollars for every such offence, by the court having jurisdiction. When the fine shall have been collected, as in other cases, the amount shall be divided, one-half to the informer, the other half to the county Treasury, for county purposes.

Approved, March 18, 1858.

C. HARRIS, *Governor.*

A Resolution to Adjourn.

Be it resolved by the Legislature of the Chickasaw Nation, That this called session of the Chickasaw Legislature adjourn, *sine die*, on Saturday, the 20th instant, at 10 o'clock, precisely.

March 19, 1858.

An Act to constitute Col. Edmond Pickens as one of the Commissioners to adjust and settle up all Chickasaw accounts with the Government of the United States, according to the Treaty of June 22, 1852.

WHEREAS, Sampson Folsom was duly authorized by an act passed the Chickasaw Financial Council on the 8th day of January, 1855, to settle up all matters relative to the meaning of the Fourth Article of the Treaty of June 22d, 1852, between the United States and the Chickasaw Nasion; and also by a subsequent act of the Chickasaw Legislature, passed February 9th, 1857, appointing James Gamble to act in conjunction with Sampson Folsom, with full power to perform all the duties required and authorized by the said act of January 8th, 1855. *And, whereas*, It becomes necessary that an additional Commissioner be appointed to act in conjunction with Sampson Folsom and James Gamble, to carry into a final effect the intention and meaning of the Fourth Article of the Treaty of June 22d, 1855; *Therefore*,

Be it enacted by the Legislature of the Chickasaw Nation, That Col. Edmond Pickens be and he is hereby constituted a Commissioner, with full and efficient power to co-operate and act in conjunction with Sampson Folsom and James Gamble, who were formerly appointed Commissioners on the part of the Chickasaw Nation, to carry into effect a final settlement with the Government of the United States, all of the unsettled business existing under treaty stipulations, as contemplated and authorized by an act passed the Financial Council, January 8th, 1855, and that of an act passed by the Legislature, February 9, 1857.

Be it further enacted, that an additional contingent fee of five per cent. is hereby allowed upon all moneys that those three Commissioners may secure to the Nation; and it is also understood, that Col. Edmond Pickens shall bear his own expenses in going to and returning from Washington, and during his stay there.

Be it further enacted, that the above act shall not be so construed as to allow more than thirty per cent. upon all moneys that those three Commissioners may secure for the benefit of the Nation.

Be it further enacted, that in case either or any of the Commissioners should die, or resign, the Governor of the Nation shall have power to appoint another competent person to fill the vacancy, by granting a commission as heretofore provided in such cases.

Be it further enacted, that if Col. Edmond Pickens, in conjunction with James Gamble and Sampson Folsom, gain any money from the United States in the settlement of the unsettled claims against the United States, shall, after deducting the thirty per cent., receive and receipt for the balance; and if there be more than fifty thousand dollars, they shall invest it in United States stock for the benefit of the Chickasaw Indians; and if there be fifty thousand dollars, or less, they shall turn it over to the Chickasaw Agent for him to bring out to the Nation.

Be it further enacted, that the Delegates or Commissioners are hereby authorized to receive and receipt to the Government of the United States for any sum of money not to exceed twenty thousand dollars; the money to be taken out of any moneys due the Chickasaw Indians, as interest money from the Government of the United States, *provided* that the Commissioners do not get any money on the claims against the United States, they are authorized to receipt for that amount; or, if they do gain or get any money on the claims, and the amount is less than twenty thousand dollars, they are empowered to draw from any interest money due the Chickasaw Indians, a sufficient amount to make the sum of twenty thousand dollars.

Be it further enacted, that should the Commissioners succeed in the prosecution of said claims, they are required to remit said amount of twenty thousand dollars to the Nation, by the United States Agent for the Choctaws and Chickasaws; and if not, said amount shall be drawn as above directed, and placed in the hands of said agent, and by him to be placed in the National Treasury for National purposes.

Approved, March 19, 1858.

C. HARRIS, *Governor.*

A Resolution in relation to Printing the Laws.

Be it resolved by the Legislature of the Chickasaw Nation, That the Governor be and he is hereby authorized to request J. T. Daviess to publish all the acts of the present called session of the Legislature, and present his account to the October session, 1858.

Approved, March 20, 1858.

C. HARRIS, *Governor.*

An Act in relation to Divorces.

Be it enacted by the Legislature of the Chickasaw Nation, That the several District Courts of this Nation shall hear and determine suits for the dissolution of marriages. The courts aforesaid are hereby invested with full power and authority to decree divorces from the bonds of matrimony, in the following cases; that is to say, in favor of the husband where the wife shall have been taken in adultery, or where she shall have voluntarily left his bed and board for the space of six months with the intention of abandonment; and also in favor of the wife for the same offences.

Be it further enacted, that a divorce from the bonds of matrimony may be decreed in the following cases: where either the husband or wife is guilty of excesses, cruel treatment, or outrageous towards the other, if such ill-treatment is of such a nature as to render their living together insupportable.

Be it further enacted, that in all suits and proceedings from the bonds of matrimony the defendant shall not be compelled to answer upon oath, nor the petition taken for confessed, for want of an answer, but the decree of the court shall be rendered upon full and satisfactory evidence independent of the confession of either party, and upon the verdict of a jury affirming the material facts alleged in the petition. The court pronouncing a decree of divorce shall also decree and order a division of the estate of the parties in such way as may seem just and right, having due regard to the rights of each party and their children, if any ; *Provided*, *however*, nothing herein contained shall be construed to compel either party to divest him or herself of the title to real estate or slaves.

Be it further enacted, that a divorce from the bonds of matrimony shall not in anywise affect the legitimacy of the children thereof; and it shall be lawful for either party after the dissolution of the marriage to marry again.

Be it further enacted, that either party may take depositions of witnesses under the same rules and regulations as exist in other suits, and that either party may obtain an appeal to the Supreme Court, from any decree, in the same manner as other suits.

Be it further enacted, that on and after the day on which the action for divorce was brought, it shall not be lawful for the husband or wife to contract any debts on account of the community property, nor to dispose of the lands or slaves belonging to the same ; and any alienation by either after that time shall be null and void, if it be proved to the satisfaction of the Judge and jury that such an alienation was made with a fraudulent view of injuring the rights of the other.

Be it further enacted, that should there be any outstanding debts against the parties previous to the time that the dissolution is granted by the court, each party shall be equally bound to settle such debt or debts.

Be it further enacted, that it shall be the duty of the presiding Judge, in a case of divorce, to assess the cost of the suit on the party that loses the suit, and the costs shall not be less than twenty-five nor exceeding fifty dollars, at the discretion of the court.

Be it further enacted, that the costs of all divorces shall be collected by the sheriff or constable, and placed in the County Treasury, for public purposes.

Be it further enacted, that when a man and wife wish to be dissolved from the bonds of matrimony, and they both appear in open court and claim to be dissolved, it shall be the duty of the presiding judge to grant such dissolution; and there shall be a record kept of the same in the record books of the court, and there shall be no costs assessed against either party.

Approved, March 20, 1858.

C. HARRIS, *Governor.*

Governor's Proclamation.

To the honorable members of the Legislature: I am indeed sorry to be under the necessity of calling the members of the Legislature together again; but owing to an oversight in the members of the Senate to dispense with the "Constitutional Rule" before taking up bills, they become of no effect: you will therefore please remedy this as best you can. Also, the committee on claims had not time (by your resolution to adjourn) to make out all the claims and appropriations, and report to the Legislature. I also recommend a law in regard to appeals; also a law in relation to witnesses.

C. HARRIS, *Governor.*

An Act to legalize certain Acts.

Be it enacted by the Legislature of the Chickasaw Nation, That the following acts of the called session of March, 1858, be and the same is hereby legalized to all intents and purposes, and shall remain in full force and virtue until repealed by an act of the Legislature of the Chickasaw Nation, viz:

An act in relation to slander.

An act in relation to cohabiting with negroes.

An act to take the evidence of disabled persons.

An act to fine persons who are found with whiskey.

An act in relation to the descent of property.

An act in relation to the funeral expenses of Ah-thle-yo-ubby.

An act to have all the acts of the called session of March, 1858, published.

An act appointing a delegate to Washington.

An act in relation to divorces.

An act to legalize the law in relation to ardent spirits.

An act compelling witnesses to testify in courts and before grand juries.

A resolution granting permission to J. C. Robinson to close one month earlier.

Approved, March 20, 1858.

C. HARRIS, *Governor.*

An Act legalizing the law in relation to Ardent Spirits.

Be it enacted by the Legislature of the Chickasaw Nation, That, from and after the passage of this act, the law relating to ardent spirits, &c., that was passed at the October term of the Legislature, for the year A. D. 1856, and printed in the Constitution and Laws of the Chickasaw Nation, is hereby adopted, and the same value shall be attached to it as if it had been passed by the Legislature of 1857, and it shall remain in full force and effect until it is repealed by the Legislature of the Chickasaw Nation.

Approved March 20, 1858.

C. HARRIS, *Governor.*

An Act in relation to Appeals.

Be it enacted by the Legislature of the Chickasaw Nation, That, from and after the passage of this act, any person or persons who shall wish to appeal from any of the decisions of the courts of this Nation, (with the exception of the Supreme Court,) shall file with the clerk of the court that they wish to appeal from a petition, setting forth their reasons for wishing to appeal from the judgment of the court where the case had been decided. The petition must be filed within five days after the decision of the court; and if not filed within the time prescribed, the decision shall be final, and there can be no appeal taken after that time.

Be it further enacted, that it shall be the duty of the Judge of the court where such decision was made to grant an appeal to the parties petitioning, *provided* that this act has been complied with.

Be it further enacted, that if the case be a civil case, or where the rights of property is to be tried, it shall be the duty of the sheriff or constable to keep the property in their possession for the term specified for taking an appeal; and if the appeal be granted, the defendant shall give a bond, with good and approved sureties, in at least double the amount of the value of the property in dispute, (in writing,) for the forthcoming of the property. If said defendant cannot give bond, then the sheriff or constable shall hold the property until a final disposition is made. Said bond above mentioned shall be collected, with all costs, if forfeited.

Approved, March 20, 1858.

C. HARRIS, *Governor.*

Appropriation Bill.

Be it enacted by the Legislature of the Chickasaw Nation, That the sum of eight hundred and forty-eight dollars and ninety cents is hereby appropriated out of the first money that may come into the hands of the National Treasurer, to pay the following persons the amounts that are opposite to each name:

SENATE—	Jackson Kemp, ...	$24 00
	C. S. Love, ...	24 00
	J. E. Anderson, ...	24 00
	Charley Brown, ...	24 00
	Charley Sheco, ...	15 00
	T. L. Mitchell, Secretary, ...	24 00
	G. D. James, Secretary, ...	15 00
	B. McLish, Sergeant-at-Arms, . . .	24 00
	Wm. Kemp, ...	24 00
	Ed. Pickens, ...	24 00
	Robt. Leader, ...	24 00
	J. Patterson, ...	24 00
	Capt. Parker, ...	24 00
	D. Frazier, Int., ...	15 00
	G. D. James, guarding and boarding prisoner, ...	17 50
HOUSE—	J. McCoy, ...	24 00
	Duncan Ned, ...	18 00
	A. M. M. Upshaw	24 00
	Morgan Colbert, ...	24 00
	O-kar-yam-by, ...	24 00
	Ah-shar-ho-tubby	24 00
	Wm. McLish	19 50
	J. Kemp, Interpreter, ...	21 00
	H. Colbert, Secretary, ...	18 00
	A. Harlin, stationery, ...	35 00
	C. Harris, on account of execution of Ah-thle-yo-ubby, ...	42 00
	Amount carried over . .	$600 00

	Amount brought over . .	$600 00
House—	C. S. Humes, (locks,)	2 00
	D. Colbert, ...	24 00
	B. McLauchlin, ...	24 00
	J. D. Harris, ...	18 00
	A-shar-luby	24 00
	Tah-har-tubby	24 00
	Reuben Kemp, ...	21 00
	Dr. Allen, ...	16 50
	Pa-suby, Sergeant-at-Arms, ...	24 00
	S. Humphreys, ...	34 90
	C. Harris, ...	11 50
	J. T. Daviess, ...	25 00
		$848 90

Approved, March 22, 1858.

C. HARRIS, *Governor.*

A Resolution appointing Draftsmen.

Be it resolved by the Legislature of the Chickasaw Nation, That Simon B. James and Thomas L. Mitchell be and they are hereby appointed draftsmen to draft laws and assist the constitution and law committee, when called upon by said committee, for the present session of the Legislature.

Approved, October 6, 1858.

D. COLBERT, *Governor.*

An Act authorizing the Sale of the Old Council House.

Be it enacted by the Legislature of the Chickasaw Nation, That the sheriff of Tishomingo county shall sell to the highest bidder, for cash in hand, the building in Tishomingo city, known as the Old Council House. The sale of said building shall take place at one o'clock, P. M., on Saturday, the 9th of

October, 1858, and the proceeds of said sale shall be put in the National Treasury of the Chickasaw Nation, for public purposes.

Approved, October 8, 1858.

D. COLBERT, *Governor.*

An Act fixing the Governor's Salary.

Be it enacted by the Legislature of the Chickasaw Nation, That, from and after the passage of this act, the annual salary of the Governor of the Chickasaw Nation shall be seven hundred and fifty dollars.

Approved, October 8, 1858.

D. COLBERT, *Govèrnor.*

An Act changing the time of holding the County Courts.

Be it enacted by the Legislature of the Chickasaw Nation, That from and after the first day of January, 1859, the County Judges of this Nation shall hold their courts on the third Wednesday in each and every month.

Be it further enacted, that part of the act entitled "An act to organize the County Court," which conflicts with this act, is hereby repealed.

Approved, October 9, 1858.

D. COLBERT, *Governor.*

An Act against defacing the Capitol.

Be it enacted by the Legislature of the Chickasaw Nation, That, from and after the passage of this act, any person or persons who are caught cutting, marking or in any way defacing any part of the Capitol of the Chickasaw Nation, shall be subject to a fine of not less than one dollar nor more than five thousand dollars, according to damages done said Capitol.

Be it further enacted, that the Court having jurisdiction thereof shall take cognizance of the violation of this act. All fines thus collected shall go to the National Treasury.

Approved, October 12, 1858.

D. COLBERT, *Governor.*

An Act fixing the salary of the Supreme Judges.

Be it enacted by the Legislature of the Chickasaw Nation, That the Supreme Judges of this Nation shall, for their services, each receive at the rate of two hundred dollars per annum, and that this act take effect from and after its passage; and all laws or parts of laws conflicting with this act are hereby repealed.

Approved, October 12, 1858.

D. COLBERT, *Governor.*

An Act in relation to money that may come into the hands of Supreme Judges.

Be it enacted by the Legislature of the Chickasaw Nation, That, from and after the passage of this act, any money or moneys that may originate or accumulate in the hands of the Supreme Court of this Nation for license granted or fines imposed for contempt of court, shall be paid into the hands of the National Treasurer for national purposes; and it shall be the duty of the Supreme Court to make a report of the amount of the moneys paid into the National Treasury to the Auditor of Public Accounts annually.

Provided, however, that all money or moneys that have heretofore originated or accumulated in the hands of the

Supreme Court, and that is now in the hands of the Supreme Court of this Nation, shall be paid into the hands of the National Treasurer, for national purposes.

Approved, October 12, 1858.

D. COLBERT, *Governor.*

An Act amendatory to an Act entitled "An Act prohibiting Negroes from voting and holding office."

Be it enacted by the Legislature of the Chickasaw Nation, That, from and after the passage of this act, no negro or descendant of a negro shall have any of the rights, privileges and immunities of citizens of this Nation, and shall not be allowed his oath in any of the courts of the Nation, where any other person but a negro or descendant of a negro is interested.

Be it further enacted, that any law or parts of laws conflicting with this act are hereby repealed.

Approved, October 12, 1858.

D. COLBERT, *Governor.*

An Act against Burning the Woods and Prairies.

Be it enacted by the Legislature of the Chickasaw Nation, That, thirty days from and after the passage of this act, any person or persons who shall wilfully set the woods or prairies on fire at any time between the first day of August and the first day of March shall be deemed guilty of a misdemeanor, and upon conviction thereof shall, for each and every offence, be fined in any sum not exceeding ten dollars, at the discretion of the court having jurisdiction of the same; and the said fine, when collected, one half shall go to the informer and the other half to the County Treasurer.

Be it further enacted, that in case the person is not able to pay the above fine, he shall be imprisoned in the National jail any length of time not exceeding ten days, at the discretion of the court.

Be it further enacted, that when the property of any person is injured or destroyed by means of the woods or prairies being fired, the person sustaining the damage shall make application to the County Judge, who shall appoint two competent persons to assess the damages, and if the amount so assessed does not exceed fifty dollars, the County Court shall give judgment in the case; but when the amount exceeds fifty dollars, the Circuit Court shall have jurisdiction of the same, and the offender shall be responsible for all damages, and shall be required to pay to the person sustaining the injury a full equivalent for all damages, which shall be collected in the same manner as bonds and fines.

Be it further enacted, that when the offender is not able to refund the person sustaining a damage as above required, he shall be imprisoned any length of time not exceeding one month, at the discretion of the court having jurisdiction.

Approved, October 13, 1858.

D. COLBERT, *Governor.*

An Act in relation to the Circuit Judge giving a Prisoner notice of his Trial and assigning him Counsel.

Be it enacted by the Legislature of the Chickasaw Nation, That in all criminal cases amounting to murder, felony, and larceny, it shall be the duty of the Circuit Judge to give the prisoner or person accused at least two days' notice of his trial, and in case the accused person is not able to employ counsel, the presiding judge shall appoint the said person counsel at least two days before his trial.

Be it further enacted, that any person is incapacitated from sitting on any of the above cases as a juryman, where he has expressed his opinion publicly or may be related by affinity or consanguinity within the degrees prescribed by a constitutional provision.

Approved, October 13, 1858.

D. COLBERT, *Governor.*

An Act in relation to a Wife's separate Property.

Be it enacted by the Legislature of the Chickasaw Nation, That, from and after the passage of this act, it shall be the duty of the County Clerk of each county in this Nation to provide books for the registration of the wife's separate property.

Be it further enacted, that it shall be the duty of every woman of this Nation to have the amount of their separate property recorded in the book provided for that purpose, and also the kind of property owned by her and the amount of each kind; and she shall also be required to have her private marks and brands recorded in the same book.

Be it further enacted, that the wife's separate property shall not be held responsible for the action of the husband; *Provided,* that the wife's separate property be registered according to a former requisition of this act.

Be it further enacted, that the husband cannot sell any property belonging to the wife, *Provided* this act is complied with, unless with the wife's consent; but any property belonging to the wife that is not registered according to this act, can be disposed of by the husband, and the title to such property is good, and the same may be held responsible for the husband's actions.

Be it further enacted, that it shall be the duty of the wife to have such record made within one year from the passage of this act.

Approved, October 13, 1858.

D. COLBERT, *Governor.*

An Act regulating Legislative Elections.

Be it enacted by the Legislature of the Chickasaw Nation, That in all of the Legislative elections for the different officers of this Nation, which are elected by the Legislature, shall be by joint vote of both Houses; and in case of a tie vote in any of the elections, the polls shall be immediately opened by order of the Speaker of the House, and the voting shall be kept up until one of the tied candidates gets a majority of the whole number of votes cast.

Approved, October 13, 1858.

D. COLBERT, *Governor.*

A Bill providing for the humane treatment of Slaves, and prohibiting the introduction of Negroes guilty of high crimes.

Be it enacted by the Legislature of the Chickasaw Nation, That if any person or persons shall wilfully and maliciously murder any slave, or so cruelly treat the same as to cause death, the same shall be punished as in other cases of murder.

Be it further enacted, that if any person or persons shall knowingly introduce into this Nation any slave or slaves who have committed high crimes in other countries, he, she, or they shall be deemed guilty of a high misdemeanor, and, upon conviction thereof before the District Court, shall pay a fine of not less than fifty nor more than five hundred dollars, or be imprisoned not less than twenty nor more than sixty days, at the discretion of the Court.

Approved, October 14, 1858.

D. COLBERT, *Governor.*

An Act in relation to Free Negroes.

Be it enacted by the Legislature of the Chickasaw Nation, That, from and after the passage of this act, it shall be the duty of the County Judge of each county of this Nation to order out of the limits of their respective counties any free negro or negroes; and if such negroes fail or refuse to go, two months after the order for their departure was given, it shall be the duty of the County Judge to order the proper officers of his county to take such negro or negroes in custody, and after giving fifteen days' notice thereof, in at least three public places in his county, proceed to sell such negro or negroes to the highest bidder for cash, the aforesaid negro or negroes, for the term of one year; and it shall be the duty of the sheriff to sell such property yearly until the negro or negroes agree to leave the jurisdiction of the Nation. The purchaser of such property is hereby secured in the title of such property for the aforesaid space of time, as much so as if the negro or negroes were or had been slaves for life.

Be it further enacted, that any moneys arising from the sales of any negro or negroes, under this act, shall be placed in the County Treasury of the county where such negro or negroes was sold, for county purposes.

Be it further enacted, that, at any time after the aforesaid two months, it shall be the duty of the sheriff or constable of the county to take such negro or negroes into custody, and to dispose of them as provided for in a previous section of this act; and if such negro or negroes move out of the Nation at or before the time prescribed in a preceding section of this act, and fail to remain out entirely, they may be taken up and disposed of as previously provided for.

Approved, October 14, 1858.

D. COLBERT, *Governor.*

An Act to repeal the old Choctaw Laws.

Be it enacted by the Legislature of the Chickasaw Nation, That all laws and parts of laws which passed the Choctaw

General Council prior to the adoption of the constitution of the Chickasaw Nation are hereby declared null and void within the limits of the Chickasaw Nation, except such laws and parts of laws as may govern any judicial proceedings commenced prior to the adoption of said constitution, as is provided for in Art. 4th of a treaty made and constituted at Washington city, between the United States, the Choctaws and the Chickasaws.

Approved, October 15, 1858.

D. COLBERT, *Governor.*

An Act providing the mode of Corporal Punishment.

Be it enacted by the Legislature of the Chickasaw Nation, That whenever the punishment for any offence in this Nation is whipping, the punishment shall be inflicted by either of the sheriffs or constables, by means of a good hickory switch.

Approved, October 15, 1858.

D. COLBERT, *Governor.*

An Act to amend an Act entitled "An Act for the election of Annuity Captains, and defining their duties."

Be it enacted by the Legislature of the Chickasaw Nation, That there shall be four captains elected, one for each county, on the second Wednesday in September next, at the several places of holding elections, who, when elected, shall hold their office two years; and that at the end of every two years thereafter there shall be an election held for captains in each county. It shall be the duty of the several captains, when elected, to register all persons in his county who are entitled to annuity; and shall also register all persons who may be living out of the Nation that are known to be entitled to Chickasaw annuity, and that may wish to register under him; and to attend at the pay table and see the annuity paid out, receive and receipt for such of their warriors that may from some cause be absent.

Be it further enacted, that the time of registering shall commence on the second Wednesday in September, and close on the first day of November in each and every year. And it shall be the duty of the captains and their clerks to meet at Tishomingo city, four days previous to the time of closing the rolls, and compare and correct them: *provided, however*, if the annuity funds should be sent out earlier, so as to require the rolls sooner, the captains and their clerks shall, by order of the Governor, meet at Tishomingo city, compare and correct the rolls, and close the register four days previous to the time of payment.

Be it further enacted, that if any person or persons shall, by their own negligence or through carelessness, be left out at the time of closing the register, he, she or they shall never be allowed back annuity. Each captain's roll shall be kept open at all times for the registering of births, from the time mentioned in the above act up to the day of closing the same; and all births that may not be reported and registered until after closing the rolls, the same shall be debarred as in cases of negligence or through carelessness.

Be it further enacted, that the captain, when elected, shall take the oath as prescribed in the constitution, to the end that he shall not register any person except those who are entitled to annuity under the Chickasaw constitution.

Be it further enacted, that each captain shall receive for his services five cents for each person he shall register, he furnishing his own clerk; and in case any vacancy shall happen, by death, resignation, or inability to discharge the duties of his office, the said clerk shall act until another captain is elected, or until the captain is enabled to take charge of his duties.

Be it further enacted, that it shall be the duty of each captain to cause the rolls to be made out and filled according to the annexed plan, placing the number of persons under its separate column according to age; but such enumeration shall take place only once in every two years, the first enumeration to commence from the second Wednesday in September next.

No.	NAMES.	Males—Heads of Families.	Females—Heads of Families.	Male children under ten years.	Female children under 10 years.	Males over 10 and under 16.	Females over 10 and under 16.	NOT HEADS OF FAMILIES. Males over 16 and under 19.	Females over 16 and under 25.	Males over 19 and under 50.	Females over 25 and under 50.	Males over 50.	Females over 50.	Total.	SLAVES. Males.	Females.

Be it further enacted, that Captain Il-la-pamby is still continued a life captain, and shall receive the same pay as other captains.

Be it further enacted, that all laws and parts of laws in conflict with this act is and they are hereby repealed.

Approved, October 18, 1858.

D. COLBERT, *Governor.*

An Act authorizing the Supreme Judges to issue Law Licenses.

Be it enacted by the Legislature of the Chickasaw Nation, That, from and after the passage of this act, all persons wishing to plead law in the courts of this Nation shall be required to obtain license before they can be admitted to the bar.

Be it further enacted, that the Supreme Judges be and they are hereby authorized to issue license to any citizen whom they may deem possessed of sufficient law knowledge to practice in all the courts of this Nation.

Be it further enacted, that each applicant shall be required to pay a fee of fifteen dollars for such license to the Judge issuing the same.

Be it further enacted, that the Supreme Judges are hereby required to account for all such fees, annually, to the National Auditor.

Approved, October 18, 1858.

D. COLBERT, *Governor.*

An Act to have the Laws Translated and Printed.

Be it enacted by the Legislature of the Chickasaw Nation, That James Gamble and Joel Kemp be and they are hereby appointed to translate all the laws of the Chickasaw Nation into the Chickasaw language.

Be it further enacted, that they shall be required to translate said laws as soon as possible.

Be it further enacted, that said Kemp and Gamble shall receive for their services, out of any money in the National Treasury not otherwise appropriated, three dollars per day, each, while so engaged.

Be it further enacted, that said gentlemen shall also prepare the translation of the Chickasaw constitution for the press, and one of them shall superintend the printing of the laws and constitution.

Be it further enacted, that the said Kemp and Gamble be required to have (200) two hundred copies printed of their translation; and they are hereby authorized to make a contract with J. T. Daviess, printer, at Tishomingo city, for printing the same, and their accounts shall be brought in at the next regular session of the Legislature for the translation and for having them printed.

Be it further enacted, that the Governor be and he is hereby authorized and empowered to distribute one copy of the translated laws gratuitous to each and every male citizen of the Chickasaw Nation who can read the Chickasaw language; and if there should be an overplus, the Governor shall sell them for one dollar each, and place the funds in the National Treasury, for public purposes.

Approved, October 20, 1858.

D. COLBERT, *Governor.*

An Act to enlarge Bloomfield Academy.

Be it enacted by the Legislature of the Chickasaw Nation, That the Bloomfield Academy be enlarged so as to admit and provide for sixty students, and that the Superintendent of Public Schools for the Nation be and is hereby authorized to have the necessary improvement made for the admission of the sixty students by the opening of the session for the year 1859.

Be it further enacted, that there be and is hereby appropriated the sum of one thousand dollars out of any moneys that may be due the Chickasaws from the United States, for the year A. D. 1859, to carry on and enlarge the buildings by the time specified in the first section of this act.

Approved, October 20, 1858.

D. COLBERT, *Governor.*

An Act appointing Commissioners to amend the Contract for the Birnie Institute.

Be it enacted by the Legislature of the Chickasaw Nation, That George D. James is hereby authorized and appointed as a commissioner on the part of the Chickasaw Nation to act in conjunction with the Superintendent of Public Schools, to alter, change or amend the existing contract with the Cumberland Presbyterian Board of Foreign and Domestic Missions for Birnie Female Academy and the Chickasaw Nation; and the commissioners on the part of the Nation are required to have the alteration or amendment made as soon as possible, and they shall make a report of their proceedings in the affair at the next regular session of the Legislature.

Approved, October 20, 1858.

D. COLBERT, *Governor.*

An Act appropriating $25,000 *to the Birnie Institute.*

Be it enacted by the Legislature of the Chickasaw Nation, That the balance of the annual appropriation of three thousand dollars now due the Birnie Institute for conducting and carrying on said Institute, amounting to two thousand five hundred dollars, is hereby appropriated as an improvement fund to erect a suitable school house, meat house, corn cribs and stables, and to make any other necessary improvements that is actually necessary for the improvement of said Institute.

Be it further enacted, that Calvin S. Love is hereby appointed to act in conjunction with the Superintendent of Public Schools for the Nation, and it shall be their duty to have the necessary improvements made at this Institute; and when there is any materials furnished or work done, it shall be their duty to inspect such material furnished or work done, and, upon being satisfied with such, they shall give jointly an order on the Auditor of Public Accounts for the amount due; and the Auditor is hereby authorized to issue a warrant on the National Treasurer for the amount, and it shall be the duty of the Treasurer to pay the warrant upon its presentation.

Be it further enacted, that the building committee for this Institute be and is hereby required to keep an item account of all the work done and the cost of such work, and they shall be required to make a report of the same at the next regular session of the Legislature.

Approved, October 20, 1858.

D. COLBERT, *Governor.*

An Act to clothe the Children at the different Schools.

Be it enacted by the Legislature of the Chickasaw Nation, That the sum of two thousand and sixty-seven dollars and seventy-four cents be and is hereby appropriated out of any moneys due the Chickasaws from the United States for the year A. D. 1859, for the purpose of clothing the students at the Chickasaw Manual Laboring School, Colbert's Institute, and Bloomfield Academy, for the scholastic year of 1858.

Be it further enacted, that the sum of twelve hundred dollars, out of the amount appropriated in section first of this act, is hereby set apart for the clothing of the students at the Chickasaw M. L. Academy.

Be it further enacted, that the sum of seven hundred and twenty dollars, out of the amount in section first of this act, is hereby set apart for the clothing of the students at Colbert's Institute.

Be it further enacted, that the balance of the money appropriated in section first of this act, amounting to one hundred and forty-seven dollars and seventy-four cents, and the three hundred and ninety-two dollars and twenty-six cents, unexpended, out of the appropriation made last year to this academy, making in all five hundred and forty dollars, is hereby set apart for clothing the students at Bloomfield Academy.

Be it further enacted, that the superintendents of the aforesaid schools are hereby authorized, individually, to expend the amount of money appropriated by this act for their respective academies, to the purchase of suitable and substantial clothing that is adapted to the seasons of the year, and to their respective academies. And it shall be the duty of each superintendent to keep an item account of the amount of clothing furnished to each student, giving to each one the rates of twelve dollars' worth; and they are further required to make a quarterly report of the amount furnished to each student for the past quarter to the School Superintendent of Public Schools for the Nation.

Be it further enacted, that the School Superintendent on the part of the Nation is hereby required to examine the quality of the material furnished by each one of the academies for clothing their respective students.

Be it further enacted, that the School Superintendent is hereby authorized to give to each one of the superintendents of their schools, a certificate of the amount appropriated for their respective institutions for the purposes aforementioned.

Be it further enacted, that the different superintendents shall not issue to any of their students any clothing only a they may from time to time think actually necessary for the comfort of the student; and when any of the students have used up the amount of twelve dollars' worth, the superintendent shall send the parent or guardian of such student word that he or she has used up the amount of their appropriation.

Be it further enacted, that if this act is not strictly complied with, it shall be the duty of the Superintendent of Public Schools to report the same, and there shall be retained one-third of their respective appropriations as a forfeiture.

Approved, October 20, 1858.

D. COLBERT, *Governor.*

An Act making Albert Love an heir-at-law of Robert Love.

Whereas, there was a petition laid before the present session of the Legislature, by Mr. Robert Love, a native Chickasaw, to have Albert Love, a child of his present wife by a former husband, adopted as one of his legal bodily heirs; Therefore,

Be it enacted by the Legislature of the Chickasaw Nation, That, from and after the passage of this act, the child known as Albert Love, son of Gabriel Love, deceased, by Sarah Love, present wife of Robert Love, be and the same is hereby adopted as one of the legal representatives of Robert Love, and shall be entitled to all the rights, privileges and immunities of one of his own bodily heirs; and in case the said Robert Love dies intestate, the aforesaid Albert Love shall be considered as one of the heirs of Robert Love, and he shall be entitled to have an equal right with the bodily heirs of the aforesaid Robert Love's estate.

Approved, October 21, 1858.

D. COLBERT, *Governor.*

An Act for appointing Clerks pro tem.

Be it enacted by the Legislature of the Chickasaw Nation, That in case the clerks of any of the courts of this Nation shall from any cause be absent from the court ground at the regular terms of any of the courts, it shall be the duty of the presiding judge to appoint a clerk pro tem., who shall take the regular oath of office and shall be entitled to serve as clerk for that term only, and for such services he shall receive three dollars per day.

Be it further enacted, that when it so happens that the clerk is absent from the court ground it shall be the duty of the presiding judge to send the sheriff or constable belonging to that county after all the necessary books and papers belonging to that office, and the books and papers belonging to that office shall be turned over to the clerk pro tem., who shall keep them in custody for the term that he was appointed for; and after the court adjourns he shall turn the books, papers, and the proceedings of the court, over to the judge, who shall dispatch them to the regular clerk by one of the proper officers of that court.

Be it further enacted, that it shall be the duty of the judge to give to the clerk pro tem. a certificate certifying the number of days that he served, and, upon the presentation of such certificate, the Auditor of Public Accounts shall issue a warrant on the National Treasurer for the amount, and the Treasurer shall pay the said warrant out of any money that may be in the National Treasury unappropriated.

Be it further enacted, that, at the next term of the court from the one that the clerk was absent from, the judge shall call on the clerk to show cause of his non-attendance, and if no good and satisfactory reason for such non-attendance being shown to the satisfaction of the judge, he (the clerk) shall forfeit the sum of five dollars per day for every day that he may be absent from his duties, and the money shall be deducted out of his annual salary and placed in the National Treasury, for public purposes.

Approved, October 21, 1858.

D. COLBERT, *Governor.*

An Act to prohibit Ball Playing on the Sabbath.

Be it enacted by the Legislature of the Chickasaw Nation, That when any person or persons are caught playing ball or horse racing on the Sabbath, shall be guilty of a misdemeanor, and, upon conviction thereof before the County Court of the county where the offence was committed, shall be fined five dollars for each and every offence.

Be it further enacted, that in case any negro or negroes shall be guilty of the aforementioned offences, it shall be the duty of any person to give such negro or negroes twenty-five lashes for every time that he is caught committing the above offences.

Be it further enacted, that all fines collected under the first section of this act shall be placed in the County Treasury for county purposes.

Approved, October 21, 1858.

D. COLBERT, *Governor.*

An Act appropriating $1,141 15 *to pay the Members pro rata.*

Be it enacted by the Legislature of the Chickasaw Nation, That the sum of eleven hundred and forty-one dollars and fifteen cents, now in the National Treasury, is hereby appropriated to pay the members of the present session of the Legislature, and the clerks, sergeants-at-arms, draftsmen and interpreters; and the aforesaid amount shall be paid out *pro rata* among the aforementioned persons.

Be it further enacted, that the treasurer is hereby required to pay out the money above appropriated in such a manner that each member and each person shall have the same amount paid to them according to the amount due each one.

Be it further enacted, that the sum of one hundred dollars and fifty cents, the proceeds of the sale of the old Council House, be added to the above appropriation and be used in like manner.

Approved, October 21, 1858.

D. COLBERT, *Governor.*

An Act to change the Court Ground in Panola County.

Be it enacted by the Legislature of the Chickasaw Nation, That, from and after the passage of this act, the County and

Circuit Court ground and place of holding elections in Panola county is hereby removed and located at a place known as Black Jack Grove, about one mile east of the place known as On-tah-bit-tullah Spring Court ground; and the place shall be called Black Jack Court Ground.

Approved, October 21, 1858.

D. COLBERT, *Governor.*

An Act to suppress Rioting at Public Places.

Be it enacted by the Legislature of the Chickasaw Nation, That, from and after the passage of this act, any person or persons who shall be guilty of any riotous proceedings at any public place, or place of religious worship, or shall bring any intoxicating liquors at any of the aforementioned places, shall be guilty of a misdemeanor, and upon conviction thereof shall be fined in any sum not exceeding ten dollars; and it shall be the duty of any of the sheriffs or constables of this Nation to take such offenders into custody and keep them until they desist from such disturbances; and it shall also be their duty to inform upon such offenders to the County Judge of the county where such disturbance was acted.

Be it further enacted, that in case there shall be no sheriff or constable present when such riotous proceedings are acting, it shall be the duty of any person to take such offender into custody and shall prevent such offender from disturbing the harmony of the place; and the person taking such riotous person into custody shall inform the County Judge of the county where such disturbance was acted.

Be it further enacted, that all fines collected under the above act shall be placed in the County Treasury, for county purposes.

Approved, October 21, 1858.

D. COLBERT, *Governor.*

An Act to change the Colbert Institute into a Male School.

Be it enacted by the Legislature of the Chickasaw Nation, That, *Whereas* the Colbert Institute, under the present contract between the Board of Missions of the Methodist Church South and the Board of Public School Trustees, is a mixed school of males and females, which has been the cause of petty annoyance and trouble, it is hereby proposed, that the school may go on harmoniously, the National School Superintendent is hereby authorized and empowered, on the part of the Nation, to make a change in said contract with the proper agent or agents of the aforesaid Board of Missions, from a mixed school to a male school, and to make such other changes as he may deem beneficial to the Nation.

Approved, October 20, 1858.

D. COLBERT, *Governor.*

An Act in relation to Attachments.

Be it enacted by the Legislature of the Chickasaw Nation, That, from and after the passage of this act, the sheriff or constable of one county may serve any process, writ or attachment emanating from his county on the person of any one in another county of this Nation; and the person that may be so attached can be carried to the county where his presence is required, by the sheriff or constable serving such attachment, writ or process.

Approved, October 22, 1858.

D. COLBERT, *Governor.*

An Act to amend an Act entitled "An Act relating to Elections."

Be it enacted by the Legislature of the Chickasaw Nation, That, from and after the passage of this act, the polls for the general election by the people shall be opened at 8 o'clock, A. M., or as soon as practicable, and be closed at 5 o'clock, P. M.; and in case there is a tie between any two or more of the candidates, the polls shall be opened immediately for the purpose of deciding which one of the tied candidates are elected, and the polls of the second election shall be closed at 12 o'clock, P. M.

Be it further enacted, that any law or parts of laws conflicting with this act is hereby repealed.

Approved, October 22, 1858.

D. COLBERT, *Governor.*

An Act to preserve Bills, &c., passed by one House only.

Be it enacted by the Legislature of the Chickasaw Nation, That, from and after the passage of this act, it shall be the duty of the Secretary of the Senate, and the Clerk of the House of Representatives, at the close of each session, to collect all petitions, memorials and bills, that may have passed one House and not the other, and all other papers that may have been in their charge during the sitting of the Legislature, and turn them over to the National Secretary, to be by him safely kept in his office for future references.

Be it further enacted, that this shall not be so construed as to mean the rejected bills; but only such bills as may have passed one House, and by reason of an adjournment it never had time to be brought up.

Approved, October 22, 1858.

D. COLBERT, *Governor.*

An Act to curtail the salary of the Supreme Clerk.

Be it enacted by the Legislature of the Chickasaw Nation, That the salary of the Supreme Clerk shall be curtailed fifty dollars; and the same shall be placed upon the salaries of the Circuit and County Court Clerks *pro rata.* And that this act take effect from and after its passage; and all laws and parts of laws conflicting with this act are hereby repealed.

Approved, October 22, 1858.

D. COLBERT, *Governor.*

An Act for the relief of Geo. D. James.

Be it resolved by the Legislature of the Chickasaw Nation, That the sum of thirty-one dollars is hereby appropriated out of any money thet may be placed in the hands of the Treasurer, that is not otherwise appropriated, for a balance due G. D. James for services as Auditor from the 15th of September, 1857, up to the 20th of October, 1857.

Be it further enacted, that the Auditor of Public Accounts is hereby authorized to issue his warrant accordingly.

Approved October 22, 1858.

D. COLBERT, *Governor.*

An Act to furnish a Table for Auditor's Office.

Be it enacted by the Legislature of the Chickasaw Nation, That the sum of five dollars be and the same is hereby appropriated out of any money not otherwise appropriated, now in the hands of the Treasurer, to pay H. McKinney for one table for Auditor's Office.

Approved, October 22, 1858.

D. COLBERT, *Governor.*

An Act in relation to Schools.

Whereas, there is a Local Trustee appointed to each one of the Public Schools of this Nation, and being one of the duties of the Superintendent of Public Schools to visit each one of the Academies quarterly, and as a semi-annual visit is all that is requisite ; Therefore,

Be it resolved by the Legislature of the Chickasaw Nation, That the Superintendent of Public Schools is hereby requested to visit each one of the Public Schools of this Nation semi-annually ; once in three months after the opening of the schools, and again within one month of the close of the schools, or at the examinations.

Be it further enacted, that the Local Trustees shall visit each one of their respective schools, and shall note the progress made at each one of their schools ; and in case that the presence of the Superintendent is actually necessary at any of the schools between his regular visits, the Local Trustee for the school shall notify the School Superintendent through the sheriff or constable of his county, that he is wanted, and that his presence is needed : he shall attend such summons immediately after delivery.

Be it further enacted, that all laws and parts of laws conflicting with this act are hereby repealed.

Approved, October 22, 1858.

D. COLBERT, *Governor.*

An Act authorizing the appointment of Commissioners to meet the Cherokees, Creeks, and Seminoles, to make International Laws.

Whereas, there is a necssity for enacting some international laws between the Cherokees, Creeks, Seminoles, and the Chickasaws, in relation to any depredation that may be done in one Nation, and the offenders fleeing into the jurisdiction of either of the other Nations ; Therefore,

Be it resolved by the Legislature of the Chickasaw Nation, That the Governor be and he is hereby authorized and empowered to request the Cherokees, Creeks, and Seminoles, to meet the Chickasaws in General Council, to enact such laws that may be required to perpetuate the peace and harmony that prevails at present among the afore-mentioned tribes. And he shall also suggest the time and place of meeting. And he shall appoint six competent citizens of the Chickasaw Nation to meet the like number from each one of the other tribes, to enact such laws as the wisdom of the Council may suggest to accomplish the purpose herein set forth.

Be it further enacted, that the Commissioners appointed on the part of the Chickasaws shall receive three dollars per day that they may be detained at the place of meeting, and ten cents per mile in going to and returning from the place of meeting; and the commissioners shall pay their own expenses in going to and returning from the place, and during their stay.

Approved, October 22, 1858.

D. COLBERT, *Governor.*

An Act for the Relief of P. M. Fletcher.

Be it enacted by the Legislature of the Chickasaw Nation, That the sum of thirty-one dollars be appropriated out of any money that may be due the Chickasaws from the United States for the year A. D. 1858, to pay Peter M. Fletcher, for services rendered as School Superintendent from the 15th of September until the 24th of October, 1857.

Approved, October 22, 1858.

D. COLBERT, *Governor.*

An Act to pay out certain money as an Annuity.

Be it enacted by the Legislature of the Chickasaw Nation, That the U. S. Agent is hereby authorized, after deducting the amount of the appropriations made by the October session of the Legislature of 1858, to pay out the residue of the money that may be in his possession, belonging to the Chickasaws, due from the Government of the United States as interest money, as an annuity for 1858.

Approved, October 22, 1858.

D. COLBERT, *Governor.*

A Resolution in relation to printing the Laws.

Be it resolved by the Legislature of the Chickasaw Nation, That Thomas L. Mitchell and James N. McLish be and they are hereby appointed to make a contract with J. T. Daviess to print all the laws and resolutions passed at the present session of the Legislature, October 22, 1858. They are required to make the contract immediately after the adjournment of the present Legislature.

Approved October 22, 1858.

D. COLBERT, *Governor.*

Appropriation Bill.

To the Hon. members of the Senate and House of Representatives of the Chickasaw Nation.

SIRS—Your Committee to whom you referred the Financial account of the Nation, would most respectfully beg leave to lay before your honorable body our report.

The amount of deposite in the Treasury at the end of the fiscal year ending 30th day of September, 1857, seems to have been, as per Treasurer's report, the sum of $25,554 95; since which time there has been paid out on demands from the Auditor's Office, together with other drafts issued previous to the 30th day of September, 1857, the sum of $24,513 80; leaving a balance remaining in the Treasury standing to the credit of the Nation, the sum of $1,141 15. Against which there appears the indebtedness of the Nation, amounting to $25,580 65, as per Auditor's report of date October 4, 1858, exclusive of smaller claims against the Treasury, which will be found on the annexed list, amounting to $710 11, which added to the aforesaid mentioned amount will make $26,290 76, less $1,141 15—leaving the whole amount of the indebtedness of the Nation $25,149 61; which amount we would earnestly request the Legislature to appropriate out of the interest funds arising from the invested funds now due the Chickasaws from the United States Government, and would recommend the passage of the accompanying bill. All of which is respectfully submitted.

October 21, 1858.

JAMES GAMBLE, *Chairman.*

S. McLish, for trip to Creek Nation,	$ 6 10
I. Love, boarding prisoner 58 days,	58 00
H. C. Colbert, " " ammunition,	26 50
H. McKinney, for services at Sept. Circuit C. Term,	25 00
Joel Kemp, for registering 525 persons,	26 25
Humes & Hamilton, for table cover,	4 00
R. McLish, arrearages for services, 1857,	11 50
W. Colbert, for double barrel gun,	40 00
C. & C. Herald, for publishing Laws, &c.,	42 50
Im-ma-lah, for services as constable 50 days,	41 00
Cassy Wolf, for mis-register in 1855,	20 00
On-che-ubby, " "	20 00
E. Lowman, " 1857,	12 50
R. Ubbit-un-yo-ah, " " four persons,	50 00
Mr. Martin, for table in Senate Chamber,	5 00
Dr. Un-no-yah, mis-register in 1857, five persons,	62 50
Pul-lum-my, " "	12 50
Charley Sheco, trip to Creek Council,	5 00
A. Harlan, for stationery at sundry times,	48 26
" one pair blankets for prisoner,	8 00
Holmes Colbert, for arrearages for services in 1857,	31 10
Colbert's Institute, for improvements,	46 40
T. L. Mitchell, for table, stationery, &c.,	8 00
Four Local Trustees, $25 each per annum,	100 00
	$710 11

Be it enacted by the Legislature of the Chickasaw Nation, That the sum of twenty-five thousand one hundred and forty-nine dollars and sixty-one cents be and is hereby appropriated out of the interest arising out of the invested funds in the hands of the Government of the United States, now due the Chickasaws for the year 1858. And that the U. S. Agent, Gen. D. H. Cooper, or any other proper officer of the United States having the aforementioned funds in his hands, is hereby requested to pay over to the Treasurer of the Nation the above mentioned sum of money for the use of the Nation.

Approved, October 21, 1858.

D. COLBERT, *Governor.*

Auditor's Report.

Tishomingo City, C. N.,
Auditor's Office, Oct. 4, 1858.

To his Excellency, D. Colbert:

SIR:—I herewith submit for your inspection a schedule of the indebtedness of the Chickasaw Nation for the fiscal year of 1857-58, commencing from the second Wednesday in September, 1857, up to the present time. First, including National officers; second, the five thousand dollars that was used by the November Legislature of 1857; third, the expenses of the called session of the Legislature in March, 1858, for which drafts have been issued—for reference, you will find enclosed a list of said drafts and their different amounts; fourth, the clothing of scholars; fifth, the supposed amount of jury fees (as I cannot give a correct account of all, not having received a correct list of them from the different Circuit Clerks); sixth, the expenses of the present Legislature if it lasts 21 days; lastly, sundry claims for sundry persons for services, &c., for which are no special appropriations: all of which is respectfully submitted for investigation. The above items are as follows, to-wit:

Governor's Salary,	$750 00	
National Secretary,	400 00	
Attorney General,	300 00	
Four Sheriffs,	1,200 00	
Six Constables,	1,800 00	
Four Circuit Clerks,	800 00	
One Circuit Judge,	400 00	
Four County Judges,	800 00	
National Treasurer and Auditor,	600 00	
School Superintendent,	300 00	
Three Supreme Judges,	600 00	
Supreme Clerk,	250 00	
Total National officers debt,		8,200 00
Two thousand dollars that was used of the capitol money, as you will find per resolution of the November Legislature; also three thousand dollars of the Birnie Institute, in the same resolution,	$5,000 00	
Expenses of Legislature of March 1858,	848 90	
Cothing students of the different schools,	1,100 00	
Jury Fees,	600 00	
Captains' Salaries,	250 00	
Expenses present Legislature, 21 days, thirty members,	1,890 00	
Four Sergeants-at-Arms and two Clerks,	378 00	
Incidental expenses,	100 00	
		$18,366 90
General appropriation for Colbert's and Birnie Institutes now due,	7,000 00	
Balance due Gov. Harris in 1856-7,	80 00	
Wilson Hawkins, for boarding prisoner,	8 00	
Mrs. Humphreys, " "	125 75	
Total indebtedness,		$25,580 00

The above is as near as I can make out the statement without any list to go by. It will be something less than the above, as I give it in round numbers, and some of the offices were vacant part of the time. The above is most respectfully submitted.

G. D. JAMES, *Auditor Public Accounts.*

To his Excellency, D. Colbert, Gov. C. N.

An Act authorizing the Supreme Judges to issue License to persons wishing to practice Law.

Be it enacted by the Legislature of the Chickasaw Nation, That, from and after the passage of this act, all persons wishing to plead or practice law in this Nation, shall be required to obtain license before they can be admitted to the Bar.

Be it further enacted, that the Supreme Judges be and they are hereby authorized to issue license to any person whom they may deemed possessed of sufficient law knowledge, to practice in all the courts of this Nation.

Be it further enacted, that each applicant shall be required to pay a fee of fifteen dollars for such license, to the Judge issuing the same.

Be it further enacted, that the Supreme Judges are hereby required to account for all such fees annually to the National Auditor.

Approved, October 18, 1858.

D. COLBERT, *Governor.*

An Act in relation to the attendance of Witnesses.

Be it enacted by the Legislature of the Chickasaw Nation, That, from and after the passage of this act, any person or persons whose testimony or evidence is required in any of the courts of this Nation, upon application being made to the clerk of the court where such testimony or evidence is required, he, the clerk, shall issue a subpœna or summons for the person or persons, and it shall be the duty of the sheriff or constable to serve the same, and he shall make a return of the same to the clerk of the court where such subpœna or summons emanated.

Be it further enacted, that in case the person or persons summoned refuse or fail to attend such summons, it shall be the duty of the clerk of the court to issue a writ of citation for such person or persons who refuse or fail to attend said summons; and if good and sufficient cause cannot be shown to the satisfaction of the presiding Judge for his non-attendance, he, or she, or they shall be fined in any sum not less than five nor more than fifty dollars.

Be it further enacted, that in case any person or persons refuse to obey such summons, the party or parties having such summons issued may demand a writ of attachment for the person refusing to obey such summons, from the clerk of the County Court where his presence may be required; and it shall be the duty of the sheriff or constable of the county where such summons emanated, to apprehend and bring the party or parties before the presiding Judge, where his or their testimony is, or may be, required, if to be found within the limits of the Nation.

Be it further enacted, that when any fine or fines have been assessed upon any person or persons for not complying with such summons, it shall be the duty of the sheriff or constable to collect the same of the county where such summons emanated; and when collected, he shall pay said fine into the County Treasury where the person fined may have been required to appear.

Be it further enacted, that when the testimony or evidence of any person is required at any of the courts of this Nation, and the person not being a citizen of the Nation, the person or persons requiring such testimony shall give the opposite party at least ten days' notice of the same, and he shall file with the clerk of the court where such evidence is required interrogatories, and the opposite party may file cross-interrogatories; and such evidence shall be taken before the proper officers of the county where such witness may live, and such testimony shall be certified to by the proper person to take such deposition or testimony; and when the above requirements are complied with, the same weight shall be attached as if the person were present.

Be it further enacted, that witnesses shall receive the same pay as jurors, and be paid in the same manner.

Approved, January 20, 1859.

D. COLBERT, *Governor.*

A Bill to pay Capt. Martin Shecoe.

Be it enacted by the Legislature of the Chickasaw Nation, That the sum of twenty-seven dollars and twenty-five cents, now in the hands of Capt. Shecoe, be and the same is hereby allowed him for his services in registering his company in 1858.

Approved, January 20, 1859.

D. COLBERT, *Governor.*

Appropriation Bill for 1859.

MEMBERS TO SENATE.

404.	Jackson Kemp,	12	days,	$36 00
367.	J. E. Anderson,	12	"	36 00
391.	G. M. Allen,	12	"	36 00
376.	E. Pickens,	8	"	24 00
377.	Charley Shecoe,	5	"	15 00
379.	G. D. James,	4	"	12 00
363.	C. S. Love,	4	"	12 00
381.	C. Carter,	8	"	24 00
378.	T. L. Mitchell,	4	"	12 00
370.	Isom Shayawpoo,	4	"	12 00
390.	J. N. McLish,	4	"	12 00
			Amount carried over,	$231 00

Amount brought over, $231 00

MEMBERS OF THE HOUSE.

373.	Thomas Benton,	12 days,	36 00
371.	Chi-re-ka,	12 "	36 00
389.	R. J. Humphrey,	12 "	36 00
374.	Ish Tok,	12 "	36 00
372.	Hiokillache,	12 "	36 00
366.	Lewis Newling,	12 "	36 00
380.	Ah-shar-ca-tuby,	12 "	36 00
364.	Morgan Perry,	12 "	36 00
382.	Reuben Kemp,	12 "	36 00
386.	Koh-ah,	12 "	36 00
368.	Passubby,	12 "	36 00
385.	Samuel Colbert,	8 "	24 00
387.	Enoquoche,	7 "	21 00
398.	Holmes Colbert,	11 "	33 00
375.	E. Mook,	9 "	27 00
394.	Willis, (on errand,)	2 "	6 00
388.	Bob Wilson, (on errand,)	2 "	6 00
369.	Isom, Panola Co.,	3 "	9 00
365.	Morgan Perry, (for use of,)		3 00
	1 broom for Senate,		37
	Candles,		25
393.	Harlan, stationery,		75
392.	C. Harris, (interpreter,)	5 days,	15 00
	Howard Duncan,	12 "	36 00
			$808 99

Be it resolved by the Legislature of the Chickasaw Nation, That the sum of eight hundred and eight dollars and ninety-nine cents be appropriated out of any moneys which may be placed in the hands of the Treasurer for the year 1859, to pay the expenses of the Called Session of the Legislature in January, 1859.

Approved, January 21, 1859.

D. COLBERT, *Governor.*

An Act authorizing the Governor to make a requisition upon the General Government for Five Thousand Dollars.

Be it resolved by the Legislature of the Chickasaw Nation, That the Governor be and he is hereby requested to make a requisition, in such a manner as he may think necessary, upon the Department, at the city of Washington, for the balance, five thousand dollars, due the Chickasaw people annuity of 1858, with interest.

Approved, January 22, 1859.

D. COLBERT, *Governor.*

A Resolution for Adjournment.

Be it resolved by the Legislature of the Chickasaw Nation, That the present Called Session of the Legislature, of January 10, 1859, adjourn, *sine die*, at 10 o'clock, A. M., on the 21st of January, A. D. 1859.

Resolution in relation to striking Boundary Lines.

Be it resolved by the Legislature of the Chickasaw Nation, That there be a committee of eight appointed by the Legislature—one from each county from the Senate, and one from each county from the Representative Hall—and that said committee be required to strike off and define boundary lines of each county of this Nation.

Passed the Senate, October 5, 1859.

JACKSON KEMP, *President of the Senate.*

Attest,

JOSIAH BROWN, *Secretary.*

Passed the House, October 5, 1859.

JOEL KEMP, *Speaker of the House.*

HOLMES COLBERT, *Clerk of the House.*

Approved, October 5, 1859.

D. COLBERT, *Governor.*

Be it enacted by the Legislature of the Chickasaw Nation, The following lines shall be the boundary lines of the counties of Pickens, Panola, Pontotoc and Tishomingo.

Passed the Senate, October 6, 1859.

JACKSON KEMP, *President of the Senate.*

Attest,

J. Brown, *Secretary.*

The boundary line of the counties of the Chickasaw Nation, viz.: the boundary line of the county of Panola shall commence at the mouth of Island Bayou, on the north bank of Red river; then up said Bayou to the line between the Chickasaws and Choctaws; then along said line to Blue river; then up Blue [river] to the road that leads from Fort Washitaw to Fort Smith, where it crosses Blue [river] at Andrew Colbert's; then along said road to Hatsboughor; then along the road that leads from Hatsboughor to Tiner's, where it crosses Washitaw river; then down said river to where it empties into Red river; then down said river to the beginning point.

The boundary line of the county of Pickens shall commence on the north bank of Red river, at the the mouth of Washitaw river; then up Red river to the 98th meridian line; then north along said line to where it crosses Washitaw; then down said river to the beginning point.

Amended to read thus: The boundary line of the county of Tishomingo shall commence where the road crosses Blue river that leads from Fort Washitaw to Fort Smith, at Andrew Colbert's; thence up Blue to the Fork, above the old Dragoon crossing; then up the eastern prong to the road that leads from Fort Arbuckle to Fort Smith; then along said road to the crossing of Washitaw river; then down said river to the line of the county of Panola; then along said line to the beginning point.

The boundary line of the county of Pontitoc shall commence on the east bank of Blue river, where the line crosses that runs between the Chickasaws and Choctaws; thence along said line to the Canadian river; then up said river to the 98th meridian line; then south along said line to Washitaw river; then down said river to the line of the county of Tishomingo; then along said line to the line of the county of Panola; then down said line to the beginning point.

Passed the Senate, with the amendment of the House, October 7, 1859.

J. KEMP, *President.*

Attest,

JOSIAH BROWN, *Secretary of Senate.*

Passed the House.

JOEL KEMP, *Speaker of the House.*

Attest,

HOLMES COLBERT, *Clerk.*

An Amendment to an Act entitled "An Act in relation to Trespass."

Be it enacted by the Legislature of the Chickasaw Nation, That, from and after the passage of this act, the act entitled "An Act in relation to Trespass, &c.," that was passed by the October session of the Legislature of A. D. 1857, and approved on the 9th of October, A. D., 1857, is hereby amended thus: Any person or persons who shall be guilty of trespass shall, upon conviction before the County Court of the county where the misdemeanor was committed, be fined in any sum not exceeding fifty dollars, at the discretion of the court.

And be it further enacted, that the fine thus collected shall be paid to the person intruded upon.

Be it further enacted, that if any person shall be found guilty of cutting down trees within the limits of four hundred and forty-four yards of an actual settler, without permission granted from the settler, such person shall be considered offending the first section of this act and shall be dealt with accordingly; but in all such cases it shall be the duty of the court to appoint two responsible persons to assess the damage done, but such assessment shall not exceed fifty dollars.

Passed the Senate, October 8, 1859.

JACKSON KEMP, *President.*

Attest,

J. BROWN, *Secretary.*

Passed the House,

J. T. GAINES,

Speaker of the House of Representatives.

Attest,

A. MCCOY, *Clerk of House.*

Approved, October 8, 1859.

D. COLBERT, *Governor.*

A Bill removing White Men from the Nation for refusing to attend Court when duly summoned.

Be it enacted by the Legislature of the Chickasaw Nation, That, from and after the passage of this act, if any white person who is living within the limits of this Nation, under permission or otherwise, be summoned to attend court where his evidence is material in any suit at law, either civil or criminal, and he shall refuse to attend according to such summons without a good lawful excuse, he shall be considered an enemy to the people of this Nation, and upon information being given to the Governor by the court from which such summons issued of the non-attendance of such white person, upon such information it shall be the duty of the Governor to cause such white person to be removed out of the Nation, and for ever to stay out.

Be it further enacted, that in case it is necessary the Governor shall call upon the United States Agent for assistance to cause such person to be removed out of the Nation, for a violation of a summons as provided in the first section of this act.

Passed the House, November 10, 1857.

WM. McLIGH, *Speaker, pro tem.*

Attest,

S. B. James, *Clerk of the House.*

Passed the Senate, October 8, 1859.

J. KEMP, *President.*

Attest,

J. Brown, *Secretary of the Senate.*

Approved, October 8, 1859.

D. COLBERT, *Governor.*

An Act authorizing B. F. Colbert to establish a Ferry on Red River.

Be it enacted by the Legislature of the Chickasaw Nation, That B. F. Colbert is hereby authorized to open and keep up a ferry across Red River, at his residence, about seven miles below Preston, Texas, for the accommodation of travellers, emigrants and drovers; and to secure him against the frauds generally practised by the aforesaid classes, he is hereby authorized to fence in the landing on this side of the river with a good rail fence, and he shall be allowed the privilege of putting up a gate, to be styled a ferry gate; and any person or persons wishing to cross the aforesaid river shall be required to pay their ferriage at the gate aforementioned, and any person paying at the gate cannot be made pay at the ferry; and any person that fails or refuses to pay their ferriage may be stopped anywhere on this side of the river, and be made to pay their ferriage, provided such stoppage shall take place within the jurisdiction of this Nation.

Be it further enacted, that the aforesaid B. F. Colbert shall be required to keep at all times good boats, and trusty and efficient boatmen for the accommodation of the travelling public, and he shall be responsible to any person crossing the aforesaid ferry for any damage sustained by the negligence of any of the boatmen, or the insufficiency of any of the boats.

Be it further enacted, that the aforesaid B. F. Colbert shall, for the privilege granted in the first section of this act, at all times, keep the road leading to the ferry in good travelling order and condition, and also keep the ferry landing in good and proper order; and he shall also be required to give a bond of five hundred dollars, with security, for the faithful performance of the aforementioned requirements.

Be it further enacted, that the aforesaid B. F. Colbert be and is hereby required to have a list of his rates of charges printed and posted up in a conspicuous place near his ferry, where every person crossing the ferry may see the same, and the rates of charges shall be the same as are usually charged on the same sized water courses.

Passed the House, October 19, 1858.

A. M. UPSHAW, *Speaker pro tem.*

ttest,

A. McCoy, *Clerk of the House.*

Passed the Senate, October 8, 1859.

JACKSON KEMP, *President.*

Attest,

J. Brown, *Secretary.*

Approved, October 8, 1859.

D. COLBERT, *Governor.*

An Act providing for a Jailor.

Be it enacted by the Legislature of the Chickasaw Nation, That, from and after the passage of this act, there shall be elected in Tishomingo county a jailor, who shall hold his office for the term of two years, and until his successor is elected and qualified.

Be it further enacted, that every person who may be elected to the office of jailor shall, before entering upon the duties of his office, give bond in the same amount and in the same manner and under the same regulations as sheriffs, and which shall be conditioned for the faithful performance of all such duties as may be required of him by law.

Be it further enacted, that the jailor shall be required to receive into custody and safely keep, subject to the order of the proper court, all offenders against the laws of this Nation who have been committed to his charge by any lawful officer, and also all slaves or runaway slaves that may be committed to his charge.

Be it further enacted, that the jailor shall also be required to perform all the duties incumbent on sheriffs and constables.

Be it further enacted, that whenever any person elected jailor shall neglect or refuse to give bond, and take the oath of office within twenty days after notice of his election, the office shall be deemed vacant, and the County Judge shall certify the fact to the Governor, who shall make an appointment to fill such vacancy; and after the person so appointed shall be qualified, he shall discharge the duties of jailor until the next general election day.

Be it further enacted, that the Governor be and he is hereby authorized to appoint a jailor, who shall hold his office until the general election day in 1860.

Be it further enacted, that the jailor shall receive three hundred dollars per annum out of the National Treasury, and also an addition of fifty cents per day for food for each person committed to his charge, except in cases of runaway negroes, whose bill shall be settled by the owner or the person proving said runaway negroes and taking them out of jail.

Be it further enacted, that the jailor shall have his residence within sight of the jail.

Passed the House, October 19, 1858.

A. M. UPSHAW, *Speaker, pro tem.*

Attest,

A. McCoy, *Clerk of the House.*

Passed the Senate, October 10, 1859.

J. KEMP, *President.*

Attest,

J. Brown, *Secretary.*

Approved, together with the adjoining amendment, October 10, 1859.

D. COLBERT, *Governor.*

Amendment to Jailor Bill.

Be it further enacted, that it shall be the duty of the jailor to keep the jail swept clean and have plenty of fresh water for the use of the prisoners at all times; and it shall be the further duty of said jailor to keep the keys of the National Capitol, and have the floor scoured after the adjournment of each Legislature, and keep the several rooms swept clean and put in proper order, for the use only of the Legislature at its sittings, elections, court days, or for the purpose of any religious services.

Passed the Senate, October 8, 1859.

JACKSON KEMP, *President.*

Attest,

J. BROWN, *Secretary.*

Passed the House.

WM. KEMP, *Speaker pro tem.*

Attest,

HOLMES COLBERT, *Clerk.*

An Act in relation to Marriages under Choctaw Law.

Be it enacted by the Legislature of the Chickasaw Nation, That, from and after the passage of this act, all persons that were married under the Choctaw Law, or by mutual consent of parties which lived together as man and wife six months previous to the adoption of the constitution of the Chickasaw Nation, shall be compelled by the County Judge to have the same established upon oath, and recorded in the office of the County Clerk.

Be it further enacted, it shall be the duty of the County Judges to notify the people of their respective counties of the passage of this act; any person or persons who refuse or neglect to have their marriage recorded within three months after the passage of this act, shall be compelled to pay a fine not less than five nor exceeding fifteen dollars, at the discretion of the court.

Be it further enacted, that all fines imposed under the above act be collected by the sheriff or constable, and when collected be placed in the County Treasury, for county purposes.

Passed the House.

Attest, WM. KEMP, *Speaker.*

HOLMES COLBERT, *Clerk.*

Passed the Senate, October 10, 1859.

Attest, J. KEMP, *President.*

J. BROWN, *Secretary.*

Approved, October 10, 1859.

D. COLBERT, *Governor.*

An Act to amend an Act entitled "An Act in relation to Appeals."

Be it enacted by the Legislature of the Chickasaw Nation, When there is an appeal granted, it shall be the duty of the clerk of the court to sign all papers belonging to the case, and send them to the clerk of the court to which the appeal is taken, by the sheriff or constable of the county where the case was tried.

Passed the Senate, October 10, 1859.

Attest, JACKSON KEMP, *President.*

J. BROWN, *Secretary of Senate.*

WM. KEMP, *Speaker of the House pro tem.*

HOLMES COLBERT, *Clerk.*

Approved, October 10, 1859.

D. COLBERT, *Governor.*

An Act in relation to Pickens Court—Amendment.

Be it enacted by the Legislature of the Chickasaw Nation, That, from and after the first day of January, A. D. 1860, the Circuit and County Court ground and place of holding elections in Pickens county be removed from Rock Spring to a spring on Hi-yo-wah-na Creek, known by the name of Ish-fah-lah-nah Spring; and the name of the aforesaid place of holding courts and elections in Pickens county shall be called Hi-yo-wah-na court ground.

Passed the Senate, October 11th, 1859.

Attest, J. KEMP, *President.*

J. BROWN, *Secretary.*

Passed the House as amended.

W.M. KEMP, *Speaker pro tem.*

H. COLBERT, *Clerk of the House.*

Approved, October 11, 1859.

D. COLBERT, *Governor.*

An Act to authorize the Commissioners to file exceptions to Accounts when received.

Whereas, by the 4th article of the treaty between the United States and the Chickasaw Tribe of Indians, made and concluded at Washington city on the 22d day of June, 1852, it is provided, that inasmuch as "the Chickasaws allege that in the management and disbursement of their funds by the Government they have been subject to losses and expenses which properly should be borne by the United States; with a view, therefore, of doing full justice in the premises, it is hereby agreed that there shall be, at an early day as practicable, an account stated under the direction of the Secretary of the Interior, exhibiting in detail all the moneys which from time to time have been placed in the Treasury to the credit of the Chickasaw Nation, resulting from the treaties of 1832 and 1834, and all disbursements made therefrom, and said accounts as stated shall be submitted to the Chickasaws, who shall have the privilege, within a reasonable time, of filing exceptions thereto; and any exceptions filed shall be referred to the Secretary of the Interior, who shall adjudicate the same according to the principles of law and equity, and his decision shall be final and conclusive on all concerned;" now, therefore, to the end that there may be no unreasonable delay upon the part of the Chickasaws in filing their exceptions to said accounts:

Be it enacted by the Legislature of the Chickasaw Nation, That Col. Edmund Pickens, James Gamble, and Sampson Falsom, Commissioners on the part of the Chickasaw Nation, heretofore appointed to settle the accounts and other matters between the United States and the Chickasaws, arising under the treaty of June 22d, 1852, be and they are hereby authorized and fully empowered for, in behalf, and in the name of the Chickasaws, to file any and all such exceptions as they may deem proper to such accounts, provided for under the 4th article of said treaty of 22d of June, 1852, to be stated and submitted to the Chickasaws, in as full and complete a manner as the Chickasaw people *en masse*, or the Legislature representing them, might or could do, and to submit such exceptions in the name of the Chickasaw people to the Secretary of the Interior, in accordance with the provision of the said 4th article of said treaty of June 22d, 1852; the Legislature of the Chickasaw Nation hereby ratifying and confirming all the acts of said Commissioners done in the premises.

Be it further enacted, that the aforesaid Commissioners will make a report annually to the Legislature of all their proceedings, and furnish a true copy of all exceptions made to the accounts at each sitting of the regular session of the Legislature, until finally settled.

Passed the House as amended, October 11, 1859.

Attest, WM. KEMP, *Speaker pro tem.*

HOLMES COLBERT, *Clerk of the House.*

Passed the Senate, October 10, 1859.

Attest, J. KEMP, *President.*

J. BROWN, *Secretary of Senate.*

Passed the Senate with the amendment, October 11, 1859.

Attest, J. KEMP, *President.*

J. BROWN, *Secretary.*

Approved, Oct. 12, 1859. D. COLBERT, *Governor.*

An Act in regard to number of Warrants.

Be it enacted by the Legislature of the Chickasaw Nation, That, from and after the passage of this act, the numbering of warrants on the Treasurer from the Auditor's office shall be divided into three divisions, as follows: 1st, for National officers; 2d, for members of the Legislature and for incidental expenses; 3d, for jury and witness fees. Each division shall be kept in separate books, commencing at No. 1 of each division and continuing unto the end.

Be it further enacted, that where several certificates for jury and witness fees are held by any one person, the Auditor may consolidate them and issue one warrant for the whole; but in all such cases the Auditor shall continue numbering on his list, as above specified, from one unto the end.

Be it further enacted, that the present Auditor is hereby authorized to purchase books necessary to carry this object into execution, and may draw his warrant on the Treasurer of the Nation for the payment of the same.

Be it further enacted, that all laws or parts of laws that may conflict with this are hereby repealed.

Passed the House, October 11, 1859.

WM. KEMP, *Speaker pro tem.*

Attest,

HOLMES COLBERT, *Clerk.*

Passed the Senate, October 12, 1859.

J. KEMP, *President.*

Attest,

JOSIAH BROWN, *Secretary.*

Approved, October 12, 1859.

D. COLBERT, *Governor.*

Resolution authorizing the Election of Supreme Judge and School Superintendent.

Be it enacted by the Legislature of the Chickasaw Nation, That the election of one Supreme Judge and School Superintendent take place on Saturday, the 15th inst., at 2 o'clock P. M.

Passed the Senate.

JACKSON KEMP, *President of the Senate.*

Attest,

A. McCoy, *Secretary pro tem.*

Passed the House.

JOEL KEMP, *Speaker.*

Attest,

H. Colbert, *Clerk.*

Approved, October 13, 1859.

D. COLBERT, *Governor.*

An Act in relation to granting a permit to T. G. Mobly.

Whereas, Mrs. Sarah Humphreys having rented her building, known as the tavern in Tishomingo city, to T. G. Mobly, for the term of two years;

Now, therefore, be it resolved by the Legislature of the Chickasaw Nation, that said T. G. Mobly is hereby permitted to take charge of said tavern for the purpose of entertaining travellers for the time above specified.

Approved, October 13, 1859.

D. COLBERT, *Governor.*

An Act in relation to Prosecutions.

Be it enacted by the Legislature of the Chickasaw Nation, That, from and after the passage of this act, all criminal prosecutions shall be carried on thus: "In the name and by the authority of the Chickasaw Nation. Be it remembered that at the Circuit Court in and for the county of ——, on the —— day of ——, in the year one thousand eight hundred and ——, we, the Grand Jurors, impannelled, sworn, and charged to inquire for the body of said county, by the oaths of good and lawful persons of the county aforesaid, of all treasons, and all murders, and all offenders against the laws of the Chickasaw Nation; it is presented that A. B. of the Chickasaw Nation, in the said county, a person or persons not having the fear of God before his or their eyes, but being moved and seduced by the instigation of the Devil, did with a certain ——— one C. D., in the peace of God and the Nation then and there being, feloniously, wilfully, and of his malice and aforethought, did make an assault upon C. D., then and there giving unto the said C. D. one mortal wound, and from the said wound, he, the said C. D., did die; so we, the Grand Jurors, upon our oaths aforesaid, do say that the said A. B. did feloniously, wilfully, and of his malice aforethought, did kill and murder, or did or instigate the murder, as the case may be, against the peace and dignity of the Nation."

Be it further enacted, that all larceny and felony prosecutions shall be carried on thus: "In the name and by the authority of the Chickasaw Nation. Be it remembered, that at the Circuit Court in and for the county of ——, on the —— day of ——, in the year one thousand eight hundred and ——, we, the Grand Jurors, impannelled, sworn, and charged to inquire for the body of said county, by the oath of good and lawful person or persons of the county aforesaid, of all offenders against the laws of the Chickasaw Nation; it is presented that A. B., a person of said county and Nation, did feloniously take and steal ——, the property of ——, over the value of —— dollars, and appropriated the value thereof to his own use, against the peace and dignity of the Nation.

Witnesses, C. H. E. F., *Foreman*.
N. H."

Be it further enacted, that all writs and processes shall be: "The Chickasaw Nation to the sheriff or constable of ——, greeting: You are hereby commanded to take A. B., of the Chickasaw Nation, [a person] if to be found in the Chickasaw Nation, and —— safely keep so that you may have —— body before the court to be holden on the —— day of ——, in the year one thousand eight hundred and —— ; herein fail not, but make due returns to said court." Amended to read thus: "any person or persons," as interlined.

Passed the House, and as amended, October 14, 1859.

JOEL KEMP, *Speaker.*

Attest,

C. HARRIS, *Clerk pro tem.*

Passed the Senate and with the amendment of the House, October 14, 1859.

J. KEMP, *President.*

Attest,

J. BROWN, *Secretary.*

Approved, October 14, 1859.

D. COLBERT, *Governor.*

An Act to clothe the Children at the different Schools.

Be it enacted by the Legislature of the Chickasaw Nation, That the sum of two thousand four hundred and sixty dollars is hereby appropriated out of the interest money due the Chickasaws from the United States for the year A. D. 1859, to clothe the students at Chickasaw M. L. Academy, Colbert Institute, and Bloomfield Academy, for scholastic year A. D. 1859.

Be it further enacted, that the sum of twelve hundred dollars, out of the amount of money mentioned in the first section of this act, is hereby set apart for clothing the students at the Chickasaw M. L. Academy; and that the sum of seven hundred and twenty dollars be set apart for clothing the students at Colbert Institute; and that the remainder, which is five hundred and forty dollars, is hereby set apart for clothing the students at Bloomfield Academy.

Be it further enacted, that the amount of money set forth in the first section of this act shall be expended in the same manner as was required in an act that was passed at the regular session of A. D. 1858, entitled "An act to clothe the children at the different schools."

Passed the Senate, October 13, 1859.

JACKSON KEMP, *President of the Senate.*

Attest,

A. McCoy, *Secretary pro tem.*

Passed the House, October 14, 1859.

JOEL KEMP, *Speaker of the House.*

Attest,

C. Harris, *Clerk pro tem.*

Approved, October 14, 1859.

D. COLBERT, *Governor.*

Amendment to an Act in relation to Treason.

Be it enacted by the Legislature of the Chickasaw Nation, That the fifth clause of an act in relation to treason, be amended so as to read thus: "That any person who kills another in trying to arrest the person accused of treason or any other high crime, or any misdemeanor, or in discharge of any duty required by law, or by accident or misfortune, then in that case the party accused shall be for the same fully acquitted and discharged."

Passed the House, October 14, 1859.

JOEL KEMP, *Speaker.*

C. Harris, *Clerk pro tem.*

Passed the Senate, October 14, 1859.

Attest, J. KEMP, *President.*

J. Brown, *Secretary.*

Approved, October 14, 1859.

D. COLBERT, *Governor.*

An Act in regard to Resignation.

Be it enacted by the Legislature of the Chickasaw Nation, That, from and after the passage of this act, all officers who are elected or appointed, wishing to resign, is hereby required to write out their resignation and send it to the Governor, or the National Secretary of the Chickasaws, forthwith.

Be it further enacted, etc., that when any officer shall say that he has resigned, and neglects to send his resignation to the Governor or National Secretary within ten days after he had stated that he had resigned, he shall forfeit one third of his pay that may be due him, which amount shall revert back to the National Treasury.

Be it further enacted, it shall be the duty of any person hearing an officer stating of his resignation, to make oath to the effect that it was on such a day of the month, and that it is within the time, or over, as the case may be, as prescribed by law.

Be it further enacted, that it shall be the duty of the clerks of the different counties to report to the Auditor, that a certain officer or officers have forfeited one third of their salary by not offering their resignation within ten days, as prescribed in this act.

Passed the House, as amended.

JOEL KEMP, *Speaker*.

Attest,

HOLMES COLBERT, *Clerk*.

Passed the Senate as amended, October 14, 1859.

J. KEMP, *President*.

Attest,

J. BROWN, *Secretary of Senate*.

Approved, October 14, 1859.

D. COLBERT, *Governor*.

An Act in relation to Free Negroes. [*Amendment.*]

Be it enacted by the Legislature of the Chickasaw Nation, That, from and after the passage of this act, it shall be the duty of the County Judge of each county of this Nation to order out of the limits of their respective counties any free negro or negroes; and if such negroes fail or refuse to go within two months after the order for their departure was given, it shall be the duty of the County Judge to order the proper officers of his county to take such negro or negroes in custody, and after giving fifteen days' notice thereof, in at least three public places in his county, proceed to sell such negro or negroes to the highest bidder for cash, the aforesaid negro or negroes, for the term of one year; and it shall be the duty of the sheriff to sell such property yearly until the negro or negroes, agree to leave the jurisdiction of the Nation; and the purchaser of such property is hereby secured in the title of such property for the aforesaid space of time, as much so as if the negro or negroes had been slaves for life.

Be it further enacted, that any moneys arising from the sales of any negro or negroes under this [act] shall be [put] in the County Treasury of the county where such negro or negroes was sold, for county purposes.

Be it further enacted, that, at any time after the aforesaid two months, it shall be the duty of the sheriff of the county to take such negro or negroes into custody and to dispose of them as provided for in a previous section of this act, and, failing to remain out entirely, they may be taken up and disposed of as previously provided for.

Approved, October 14, 1859.

D. COLBERT, *Governor.*

An Act in relation to Change of Venue.

Be it enacted by the Legislature of the Chickasaw Nation, That, from and after the passage of this act, every person or persons having a suit in the District Court and believing that they cannot have justice within the county where the suit is pending, by the people being prejudiced to him or them; in that case either party may petition to the judge of the court for a change of venue.

Be it further enacted, that the party or parties petitioning for a change must state their reason for wanting a change, and must verify, on signing the petition before a legal officer, that the facts therein contained are true; then, in that case, the judge shall grant a change, but not to more than two counties, provided the above act has been complied with.

Passed the Senate, October 14, 1859.

J. KEMP, *President.*

Attest,

J. BROWN, *Secretary.*

Passed the House, October 14, 1859.

JOEL KEMP, *Speaker.*

Attest,

C. HARRIS, *Clerk pro tem.*

Approved, October 14, 1859.

D. COLBERT, *Governor.*

An Act in relation to Trading with Negroes.

Be it enacted by the Legislature of the Chickasaw Nation, That, from and after the passage of this act, all and every person or persons are hereby expressly prohibited from trading with any negro or negroes, slaves, without a permit from their owners or the person having him or them in charge; and if any person or persons trade with any negro slave without a permit, he, she or they shall be deemed guilty of a misdemeanor, and upon conviction thereof shall be compelled to pay a fine of not less that fifteen nor more than forty dollars, at the discretion of the court having jurisdiction of the same.

Be it further enacted, that if any citizen from the United States shall come within the limits of the Chickasaw Nation and trade with any negro or negroes without a permit from their owner or the person having them in charge, he or they so offending shall be arrested by the sheriff or constable, or any citizen of the Nation, and taken to the United States Agent for the Chickasaws and Choctaws, to be dealt with according as the law directs.

Be it further enacted, that when the above fine is collected it shall be placed in the National Treasury, for public purposes.

Passed the House, October 15, 1859.

Attest, JOEL KEMP, *Speaker.*

C. HARRIS, *Clerk pro tem.*

Passed the Senate, October 15, 1859.

[Attest,] J. KEMP, *President.*

J. BROWN, *Secretary of the Senate.*

Approved, October 15, 1859.

D. COLBERT, *Governor.*

An Act in relation to translating the Laws.

Be it enacted by the Legislature of the Chickasaw Nation, That James Gamble be and he is hereby continued in his appointment as a translator of the Chickasaw laws into the Chickasaw language, under the same pay, duties and requirements as required of him in a previous act by a former Legislature, and shall have the privilege to appoint his own assistant, if he deem it necessary, who shall be under the same pay as Mr. James Gamble.

Be it further enacted, etc., that all laws that may be in conflict with this are hereby repealed.

Passed the Senate thus amended, October 15, 1859.

JACKSON KEMP, *President of the Senate.*

Attest, J. BROWN, *Secretary.*

Passed the House, October 17, 1859.

Attest, JOEL KEMP, *Speaker.*

HOLMES COLBERT, *Clerk.*

Approved, October 17, 1859.

D. COLBERT, *Governor.*

An Act in relation to pay Appraisers of an Estate.

Be it enacted by the Legislature of the Chickasaw Nation, That from and after the passage of this act, that the person or persons that are appointed by the County Judge to appraise the property of an estate, they shall be entitled to one per cent. each on the dollar of all the property that may be appraised, and the pay shall come out of the estate, and the County Judge shall see that the appraisers get their pay.

Approved, October 17, 1859.

D. COLBERT, *Governor.*

An Act authorizing D. H. Cooper to pay to Cyrus Harris, Treasurer, all moneys in his hands belonging to the Chickasaws since last Legislature.

Be it enacted by the Legislature of the Chickasaw Nation, That Douglas H. Cooper, U. S. Agent for the Chickasaws and Choctaws, be and he is hereby requested and authorized to turn over all moneys belonging to the Chickasaws which may have come into his hands since the last Legislature of the Chickasaw Nation, to Cyrus Harris, Treasurer of the Chickasaw Nation, for national purposes.

Approved, October 17, 1859.

D. COLBERT, *Governor.*

A Bill in relation to Burney Institute.

Be it enacted by the Legislature of the Chickasaw Nation, That if the Cumberland Presbyterian Board of Foreign and Domestic Missions should fail to have a superintendent to superintend the Burney Academy, located in Pickens county, the first day of February, 1860, that the contract existing between the Board of Trustees of Public Schools, on the part of the Chickasaws, and Samuel Corley, on the part of the Cumberland Presbyterian Board of Foreign and Domestic Missions, is hereby null on the part of the Chickasaws.

Be it further enacted, that as there are suitable buildings now ready for carrying on a school in the aforesaid county, that Joel Kemp, G. D. James and D. C. Carter be and they are hereby authorized and empowered, for and in behalf of the Chickasaw Nation, to enter into and conclude a contract with any Board, or any competent person or persons, for conducting and carrying on a female school at the Burney Institute, for the term of not less than one nor more than ten years, as the parties may agree, upon equitable terms, always keeping in view the interest of the Nation.

Be it further enacted, that the persons authorized on the part of the Chickasaws report their proceedings in the affair to the next session of the Legislature, for its approval or disapproval.

Passed the Senate, October 18, 1859.

C. CARTER, *President pro tem.*

Attest,
J. BROWN, *Secretary*,

Passed the House.

JOEL KEMP, *Speaker*.

Attest,
HOLMES COLBERT, *Clerk*

Approved, October 18, 1859.

D. COLBERT, *Governor*.

An Act in relation to paying Attorney and Judge, pro tem.

Be it enacted by the Legislature of the Chickasaw Nation, That from and after the passage of this act, that when the Judge of the District Court assigns an attorney for a prisoner, the attorney shall defend the case through all the courts of the Chickasaw Nation, and shall receive for his services twenty-five dollars, to be paid out of the National Treasury.

Be it further enacted, that where there is a Judge *pro*

tempore appointed, he shall receive two dollars per day for his services as Judge, and to be paid out of the County Treasury.

Approved, October 18, 1859.

D. COLBERT, *Governor.*

An Act to pay William Cravat for services as Supreme Judge.

Be it enacted by the Legislature of the Chickasaw Nation, That the sum of six dollars be and the same is hereby appropriated to pay William Cravat for his services as Supreme Judge, at the October Term of the Supreme Court, A. D. 1859 ; and that the Auditor is hereby required to issue a warrant on the Treasurer for the same.

Approved, October 19, 1859.

D. COLBERT, *Governor.*

An Act of Adoption.

Be it enacted by the Legislature of the Chickasaw Nation That George Washington and his Shawnee warriors, comprising one hundred and sixty-eight persons in all, as shown by schedule annexed, shall be allowed to remain in this Nation, only subject to the laws of this Nation, during good behavior.

Be it further enacted, that the said persons are not allowed, in any way, to participate in our annuity or National fund.

SCHEDULE.

	M.	W.	C.	
George Washington, - - -	1	1	6	7
Thomas Washington, - - -	1	1	2	4
Panter Hood, - - - -	7	1	5	7
John Hood, - - - -	1	1	1	3
			Carried over,	21

			Brought over,	21
Wa-yah-ka-ish-ka,	2	2		4
Fox,	1	1	7	9
Walker,	1	1	6	8
Jim,	1	1	2	4
Bear,	1	1	5	7
George Hood,	1	1	3	5
Sky Buck,	1	1	3	5
Jim Tibbow,	1	1	2	4
Law-wah-lou-wa,	1	1	2	4
George,	1	1	5	7
Ma-ish-qui-wa,	1	1	1	3
Jim Spy Buck,	1	1	3	5
Green Grass,	1		5	6
Big Shawnee,	1	2	2	5
Dickerson,	2	1		3
Mish-ha-cash,		1	3	4
Davis,	1	1	4	6
John Gibson,	1	1	3	5
Little Horn,	1	1	3	5
John Piccorn,	1	1	6	8
Quo-que-be,	1		3	4
Lewis,	1			1
Rabbit,	2	1		3
Chicken,	2	2	3	7
Charles Tibbow,	1	1	2	4
Little Jim,	1	1	8	10
Ha-qua-mah,	1	1	4	6
Teblow,		1	2	3
				168

Approved, October 19, 1859.

D. COLBERT, *Governor.*

An Act in relation to the Auditor issuing his Warrants, etc.

Be it enacted by the Legislature of the Chickasaw Nation, That the Auditor of Public Accounts is hereby authorized to issue his warrant in favor of the members of the present Legislature and its other officers, according to the list furnished by the clerks of either House of the Legislature.

Be it further enacted, that the Treasurer is hereby authorized to pay the expenses of the present Session of the Legislature out of whatever money he may have on hand not otherwise appropriated at the present, and the balance to remain in his hands until he receives the general appropriation made to meet the indebtedness of the fiscal year eighteen hundred and fifty-eight and eighteen hundred and fifty-nine.

Approved, October 19, 1859.

D. COLBERT, *Governor.*

An Act authorizing the National Secretary to make a contract with E. J. Foster to have the Laws printed, etc.

Be it enacted by the Legislature of the Chickasaw Nation, That the National Secretary be and he is hereby authorized to make a contract with Mr. E. J. Foster, printer, at Tishomingo city, C. N., to have printed sixty copies of all the laws passed at the present session of the Legislature, together with all laws and parts of laws that may be found in his office that may have passed in the Legislature at the present session of 1858, and the Called Session of 1859, at an early day as practicable, for the use of the officers and translators of the Nation, and other purposes.

Be it further enacted, that the said Foster be requested to make out his account and present it to the Auditor of Public Accounts, who is hereby authorized to issue his warrant on the National Treasurer for the payment of the same out of any unappropriated money that may be in the hands of the Treasurer belonging to the Chickasaws.

Approved, October 20, 1859.

D. COLBERT, *Governor.*

An Act in relation to appropriating Six hundred dollars to pay the expenses of Delegates to the Creek Council.

Be it enacted by the Legislature of the Chickasaw Nation, That the sum of six hundred dollars is hereby appropriated out of any unappropriated money that may be in the hands of the National Treasurer belonging to the Chickasaws, for the purpose of defraying the expenses of six Delegates to the Creek Council, to commence on the 6th day of November, 1859, and that the Auditor of Public Accounts be and he is hereby authorized to issue his warrants in favor of such persons as may have been appointed by the Governor to attend said Creek Council.

Be it further enacted, that in case any of the Delegates so appointed should, in case of sickness or inability, fail to attend said Council, the warrant issued to such person failing to attend shall not be paid.

Be it further enacted, that the National Secretary be and he is hereby requested to furnish the Auditor with a list of persons appointed as Delegates to the said Creek Council.

Approved, October 20, 1859.

D. COLBERT, *Governor.*

An Act in relation to the County Judges appointing Patrol.

Be it enacted by the Legislature of the Chickasaw Nation, That, from and after the passage of this act, it shall be the duty of the County Judges of the different counties to appoint four men in each county to act as patrol, to keep down all disorderly conduct which may be committed by negroes roving about through the country without a pass from the owners. The said patrol shall be required to ride three times a week, and shall receive four dollars a month for such services, and to be paid out of the County Treasury.

Be it further enacted, that if any negro slave is caught from home without a pass, or a permit to trade, from their owners, or the person having them in charge, he, she or they shall receive thirty-nine lashes on their bare back, by the patrol or any citizen of the Nation.

Be it further enacted, that the County Court shall appoint the patrol where they will be of the most benefit to the county, and he shall notify them of their appointment, and they are required to meet at the County Court and elect two captains, and adopt some rules and the length of time a pass is to last, and the County Judge shall administer the oath to the patrol, and it shall extend to the faithful performance as patrol.

Approved, October —, 1859.

D. COLBERT, *Governor.*

An Act to pay the Annuity of 1859.

Be it enacted by the Legislature of the Chickasaw Nation, That after the U. S. Agent, or any other proper officer, shall have paid to the National Treasurer the sum of twenty-two thousand nine hundred and fifty dollars and fifty-four cents, the balance remaining in his hand shall be paid out as an annuity for 1859.

Approved, October 20, 1859.

D. COLBERT, *Governor.*

An Act appropriating pay to Christopher Columbus as Supreme Judge.

Be it enacted by the Legislature of the Chickasaw Nation, That an appropriation of four dollars be and the same is hereby appropriated to pay Christopher Columbus for two days' services rendered as Supreme Judge at the October term of the court in 1858, and that the Auditor is hereby authorized to issue a warrant on the Treasurer for the same.

Approved, October 20, 1859.

D. COLBERT, *Governor.*

An Act authorizing an Agent, D. H. Cooper, on the part of the Chickasaw Reserves.

Whereas, under the stipulations contained in article 4th of the treaty between the United States Government and the Chickasaw Nation, concluded October the 20th, 1832, and those contained in articles 5th, 6th, 7th, 8th and 10th of the treaty between said parties concluded May the 24th, 1834, certain reservations of land were secured to different classes of Chickasaws therein mentioned ; and, whereas, it is believed that in numerous instances great irregularity, and, in some cases, frauds have been practised in obtaining transfers from said reserves of the lands secured to them as above stated ; and, whereas, the Secretary of the Interior has decided that, in his opinion, the United States Government is not bound under the provisions of the 3rd article of said treaty of May 24th, 1834 to prosecute suits and pay the expenses thereof for the recovery of lands or the value thereof claimed by Chickasaws, when the parties in possession hold the same under color of title from the reserves, their heirs and legal representatives ; and, whereas, the interests of the Chickasaw reserves, their heirs and legal representatives, under said treaties of 1832 and 1834, require that a full and careful investigation of everything connected with the location, sale, transfer and present value and condition of said reservations, secured, or intended to be secured by said treaties of 1832 and 1834, to members of the Chickasaw Tribe of Indians, should be had, and that in all cases where it shall appear upon investigation that the property of any Chickasaw reserve, or his heirs or legal representatives, has been improperly, fraudulently or without a full and fair consideration obtained, covertly or otherwise, by any person or persons, suit or suits should be instituted, or such other steps taken for the recovery of such property, or a just and fair compensation and remuneration therefor, as may be more conducive to the interests of such Chickasaws as have been thus unfairly, fraudulently or otherwise illegally deprived of their property : Therefore,

Be it resolved by the Legislature of the Chickasaw Nation, That Douglas H. Cooper, U. S. Agent for the Choctaws, be and he is hereby required and authorized to institute, either personally or through such person as he may select in case his duties should render it impossible for him to personally attend to the same, a careful and thorough investigation into everything connected with the location, sale and transfer of all reservations secured, or intended to be secured to any and all members of the Chickasaw Tribe under and by virtue of the treaties of 1832 and 1834 between the United States and the Chickasaw Nation; to take all legal steps which may become necessary to recover possession of any and all lands, or a just and fair compensation, remuneration or indemnity therefor, which may have been irregularly, wrongfully, fraudulently, illegally and without a full and adequate consideration, either covertly or otherwise, obtained from any of the Chickasaw reserves, under said treaties of 1832 and 1834.

Be it further resolved, that it is hereby recommended and enjoined by the Legislature, that all the reserves, their heirs or legal representatives, who were entitled to lands under the treaties of 1832 and 1834 before mentioned, who have not received a full and fair consideration for their lands, do execute such power of attorney or instrument of writing as may be necessary to enable D. H. Cooper,or such proper attorney or attorneys as he may select,to institute and prosecute such suits as may become necessary for the recovery of their lands, or a just and fair compensation therefor, or to compromise and settle all their claims with the occupants in possession thereof, upon such terms and condition as in the judgment of said D. H. Cooper or counsel may be most conducive to their interests, and to provide for the payment of all expenses which may be necessarily incurred in accomplishing the recovery of said land, or in obtaining compensation or indemnity for their losses, out of whatever lands or money that may be recovered for them.

Be it further resolved, that D. H. Cooper, U. S. Agent for

the Choctaws and Chickasaws be requested to withhold his certificate of approval from any and all deeds made or to be made for any lands reserved to Chickasaws under said treaties of 1832 and 1834, until it clearly appears and he is fully satisfied that the sale and transfer of such lands have been made in good faith, and that a full and fair consideration therefor has been actually paid to the rightful claimant to said lands; and, further, to take such steps as he may consider necessary and proper for the protection of their interests and according to law, or to law and equity, as may be.

Be it further resolved, that applicants for compensation, remuneration or indemnity for lands that may have been irregularly, wrongfully, fraudulently, illegally and without fair, adequate consideration, either covertly or otherwise, obtained from them, shall, before making such application under the foregoing resolution, be properly examined by the Legislature as to his or her competency or incompetency, and that such applicants are in reality recognized members of the Chickasaw Tribes; a full list of whom shall be reserved in the office of the National Secretary for future references.

And be it further enacted, that in all such cases where an application is made, the certificate of competency and recognized member of the Chickasaw Tribe, properly signed by the President of the Senate and by the Speaker of the House, properly attested, shall accompany the application.

Approved, October 20, 1859.

D. COLBERT, *Governor.*

An Act for Licensed Traders.

Be it enacted by the Legislature of the Chickasaw Nation, That, from and after the passage of this act, all persons licensed by the United States to trade within the limits of the Chickasaw Nation shall pay a moderate annual compensation to the respective Tribes, of three-fourths of a cent on the dollar's worth, or seventy-five cents on the hundred dollars' worth of all goods, wares and merchandise introduced into the country ; the assessment to be made upon the invoice of goods, wares and merchandise so introduced into the country, under oath.

Be it further enacted, that the above percentage is to be assessed for the land and timber used.

Be it further enacted, that the use of land and timber shall not be so construed as to allow any merchant to use more than a sufficient quantity of wood for fuel and for building purposes for the actual use of merchants, such as houses, and horse or cow lots.

Be it further enacted, that no merchant, licensed by the United States to trade as above specified, shall have the right to use more than three acres of land.

Be it further enacted, that this act is not to be so construed as to interfere with white persons who have married among the Choctaws or Chickasaws from having all the rights and privileges of using land and timber as if they were Indians.

Be it further enacted, that the Auditor of Public Accounts of the Chickasaw Nation is hereby authorized and made a proper person to assess and collect all moneys due from licensed traders under the provisions of this act, and turn the same over to the National Treasurer ; the same to be used for public purposes.

Be it further enacted, that the assessment and collection shall commmence so soon as this act is approved of by the United States Agent.

Be it further enacted, that the assessor and collector shall be under oath to discharge this duty to the interest of the Nation.

Be it further enacted, that it shall be the duty of all licensed traders to report to the assessor and collector, under the provisions of this act, all goods, wares and merchandise received at various times by them through the course of the year.

Be it further enacted, that the assessor and collector shall be allowed five per cent. out of all moneys he may collect under this act.

Approved, October 20, 1859.

D. COLBERT, *Governor.*

Appropriation Bill, 1859.

Be it enacted by the Legislature of the Chickasaw Nation, That the sum of twenty-two thousand nine hundred and fifty-four dollars and fifty four cents be and is hereby appropriated out of the interest arising out of the invested funds in the hands of the Government of the United States, now due the Chickasaws for the year 1859 ; and the United States Agent, D. H. Cooper, or any other proper officer of the United States having the aforementioned funds in his hands, is hereby requested to pay over to the National Treasurer the abovementioned sum of money for the use of the Nation, for National purposes.

Approved, October 20, 1859.

D. COLBERT, *Governor.*

TISHOMINGO CITY, C. N.
Auditor's Office, October 3, 1859.

To His Excellency D. Colbert, Governor.

I herewith submit for your inspection, a schedule of the indebtedness of the Chickasaw Nation, for the fiscal year ending September, 1859.

First—Including National officers.

Second—Deficiency jury tickets for last year.

Third—Clothing for students at different schools.

Fourth—Improvements.

Fifth—Improvements Wapamucka Institute, by authority of the Legislature.

Sixth—Called session Legislature, January, 1859.
Seventh—Jury tickets for the present year, ending September, 1859.
Eighth—Incidental expenses.
Ninth—Deficiency last year clothing B. Academy.
Tenth—Members to present session Legislature, if it lasts twenty-one days.
Eleventh—Prosecuting Attorney *pro tem.*
Twelfth—Captains' salaries.
Thirteenth—Capt. Keel's pension.
Fourteenth—Annual appropriation Burney Institute.
Fifteenth—Annual appropriation Colbert's Institute.
Sixteenth—Local Trustees.

1. Governor's salary, ...	$750 00
2. National Secretary, ...	400 00
3. Attorney General, ...	300 00
4. Four Sheriffs, $300 each, ...	1,200 00
5. Six constables, $300 each, ...	1,800 00
6. One District Judge, ...	400 00
7. Four Circuit Clerks, $212 50 each, . .	850 00
8. Four County Judges, $200 each, . .	800 00
9. One National Treasurer and Auditor, $300 each, ...	600 00
10. One School Superintendent, ...	300 00
11. Three Supreme Judges, $200 each, . .	600 00
12. One Supreme Clerk, ...	200 00
	$8,200 00

Jury fees for deficiency in appropriation last year, ...	270 90
Clothing for students at different schools, .	2,163 63
Improvements at different schools, . .	3,004 51
Called Session of Legislature, January, 1859,	808 90
Jury tickets for present year ending September,	1,242 48
Amount carried over,	$15,690 42

Amount brought over,	$15,690 42
Incidental expenses, ...	100 00
Deficiency last year's appropriation B. Academy,	100 00
Present Session Legislature, if it lasts twenty-one days, ...	2,268 00
Prosecuting Attorney *pro tem.*, . .	75 00
Captains' salaries, ...	250 00
Capt. Keel's pension, . . .	100 00
Annual appropriation Burney Institute, .	3,000 00
Annual appropriation Colbert Institute, .	4,000 00
Four Local Trustees, $25 each, . .	100 00
Three books for Auditor's office, . .	3 00
	$26,632 48
Clothing students at the different shools for 1859 and 1860, ...	$270 90

Approved, October 20, 1859.

D. COLBERT, *Governor.*

To the Legislature of the Chickasaw Nation.

We, the Committee on claims, would recommend the payment of the following claims:

		Issued.
1.	B. Kemp, board of prisoners, sixty-three days, at 50 cents per day, . . .	$34 25
	Ditto, for services, ...	1 75
2.	J. T. Davis, printing laws, 1858, . .	83 00
3.	H. C. Colbert, board of prisoners, forty-five days, at 50 cents per day, . . .	22 50
4.	Mrs. S. Humphreys, ...	75 50
5.	Mrs. S. Albertson, draft, &c., . . .	46 00
6.	C. Harris & Co., commissioner and guards, &c.,	40 00
7.	A. Alexander, board of prisoner, . .	2 00
8.	Dave or Davis, Capt., &c., of 1858, . .	6 00
9.	Jane Wilson, G. D. James' Co., . .	6 00
10.	Akahachiche, Flaphambris' Co., . . .	6 00

11.	James McCoy, table and journal, S. Court, .	9 00
12.	G. B. Hester, stationery, &c., 1858, . .	23 99
13.	T. S. Mitchell, witness fees, . . .	4 50
14.	Ahcoochamtuby, board prisoner, . .	2 00
15.	Ebahyahertuby, child's misregister, . .	6 00
16.	G. W. Allen, furnishing prisoners candles, &c.,	2 62½
17.	" board prisoner 46 days, .	23 00
19.	Emehahtuby, board prisoner 8 days, .	4 00
20.	J. A. Polson, printing message, . .	1 50
21.	G. D. James, Cir. Judge *pro tem.*, . .	10 00
22.	H. McKinney and Humphreys in behalf of prisoner, ...	1 50
23.	H. McKinney, table, paper and ink, . .	4 80
24.	W. Colbert, draft issued by Perry, . .	28 75
25.	Isom-the-opy, board prisoner, . . .	6 00
26.	Logan Colbert, jury ticket, . . .	3 20
27.	G. B. Hester, 16 jury consolidated, . .	63 05
28.	Stationery, 1859, ...	7 70
29.	G. D. James, Clerk *pro tem.*, . . .	3 00
30.	Saml. Love, Judge, ...	8 00
31.	A. McKinney, C. Judge *pro tem.*, . .	2 50
32.	Saml. Colbert, child's misregister, . .	12 50
34.	Raburn Porter and Na-jo-witer, jury fees, .	8 80
35.	Nelson Frazier, attending annuity, . .	10 50
36.	Martin Allen, ditto, . . .	10 50
37.	Like	10 50
38.	Arch. Alexander, ditto, . . .	10 50
39.	Wm. Kemp, Attorney General *pro tem.*, .	5 00
40.	C. S. Love and T. S. Mitchell, for building, .	40 00
	Duncan Ned, attending annuity, . .	10 50
	Hume & Hamilton, blanket, . . .	4 37

The above are sundry claims passed as amended, &c.

Approved, October 20, 1859.

D. COLBERT, *Governor.*

APPENDIX.

TREATIES.

CHICKASAWS.

(Concluded October 20, 1832. Ratified March 1, 1833.)

Articles of a Treaty, *made and entered into between Gen. John Coffee, being duly authorized thereto by the President of the United States, and the whole Chickasaw Nation in General Council assembled at the Council House on Pontitock Creek, on the twentieth day of October*, 1832.

The Chickasaw Nation find themselves oppressed in their present situation by being made subject to the laws of the States in which they reside. Being ignorant of the language and laws of the white man, they cannot understand or obey them. Rather than submit to this great evil, they prefer to seek a home in the west, where they may live and be governed by their own laws. And believing that they can procure for themselves a home in a country suited to their wants and condition, provided they had the means to contract and pay for the same, they have determined to sell their country and

12

hunt a new home. The President has heard the complaints of the Chickasaws, and, like them, believes they cannot be happy and prosperous as a nation in their situation and condition, and being desirous to relieve them from the great calamity that seems to await them if they remain as they are, he has sent his Commissioner, Gen. John Coffee, who has met the whole Chickasaw Nation in Council, and after mature deliberation, they have entered into the following articles, which shall be binding on both parties when the same shall be ratified by the President of the United States, by and with the advice and consent of the Senate.

Article 1. For the consideration hereinafter expressed, the Chickasaw Nation do hereby cede to the United States all the land which they own on the east side of the Mississippi river, including all the country where they at present live and occupy.

Art. 2. The United States agree to have the whole country thus ceded surveyed, as soon as it can be conveniently done, in the same manner that the public lands of the United States are surveyed in the States of Mississippi and Alabama, and as soon thereafter as may be practicable to have the same prepared for sale. The President of the United States will then offer the land for sale at public auction, in the same manner and on the same terms and conditions as the other public lands, and such of the land as may not sell at the public sales shall be offered at private sale, in the same manner that other private sales are made of the United States lands.

Art. 3. As a full compensation to the Chickasaw Nation, for the country thus ceded, the United States agree to pay over to the Chickasaw Nation all the money arising from the sale of the land which may be received from time to time, after deducting therefrom the whole cost and expenses of surveying and selling the land, including every expense attending the same.

Art. 4. The President being determined that the Chickasaw people shall not deprive themselves of a comfortable home in the country where they now are, until they shall have provided a country in the west to remove to, and settle on, with fair prospects of future comfort and happiness; it is therefore agreed to by the Chickasaw Nation, that they will endeavor, as soon as it may be in their power after the ratification of this treaty, to hunt out and procure a home for their people west of the Mississippi river, suited to their wants and condition; and they will continue to do so during the progress of the survey of this present country, as is provided for in the second article of this treaty. But, should they fail to procure such a country to remove to, and settle on, previous to the first public sale of their country here, then and in that event they are to select out of the surveys a comfortable settlement for every family in the Chickasaw Nation, to include their present improvements, if the land is good for cultivation; and if not, they may take it in any other place in the Nation which is unoccupied by any other person. Such settlement must be taken by sections. And there shall be allotted to each family as follows (to wit): To a single man who is twenty-one years of age, one section; to each family of five and under that number, two sections; to each family of six and not exceeding ten, three sections, and to each family over ten in number, four sections; and to families who own slaves, there shall be allowed one section to those who own ten or upwards, and such as own under ten, there shall be allowed half a section. If any person shall now occupy two places and wish to retain both, they may do so by taking a part at one place and a part at the other; and where two or more persons are now living on the same section, the oldest occupant will be entitled to remain, and the others must move off to some other place if so required by the oldest occupant. All of which tracts of land, so selected and retained, shall be held and occupied by the Chickasaw people, uninterrupted, until they shall find and obtain a country suited to their wants and condition. And the United States will guaranty to the Chickasaw Nation the quiet possession and uninterrupted use of the said reserved tracts of land so long as they may live on and occupy the same. And when they shall determine to remove from said tracts of lands, the Chickasaw Nation will notify the President of the United States of their determination to remove; and thereupon, as soon as the Chickasaw people shall remove, the President will proclaim the said reserved tracts of land for sale at public auction and at private sale, on the same terms and conditions as is provided for in the second article of this treaty to sell the same, and the nett proceeds thereof to be paid to the Chickasaw Nation as is provided for in the third article of this treaty.

Art. 5. If any of the Chickasaw families shall have made valuable improvements on the places where they lived and removed from, on the reservation tracts, the same shall be valued by some discreet person, to be appointed by the President, who shall assess the real cash value of all such improvements, and also the real cash value of all the land within their improvements which they may have cleared and actually cultivated at least one year in good farming order and condition. And such valuation of the improvements and the value of the cultivated lands as before mentioned shall be paid to the person who shall have made the same. To be paid out of the proceeds of the sales of the ceded lands. The person who shall value such land and improvements shall give to the owner thereof a certificate of the valuation, which shall be a good voucher for them to draw the money on, from the proper person who shall be appointed to pay the same, and the money shall be paid as soon as may be convenient after the valuation, to enable the owner thereof to provide for their families on their journey to their new homes. The provisions of this article are intended to encourage industry and to enable the Chickasaws to move comfortably. But lest the good intended may be abused by designing persons, by hiring hands and clearing more land than they otherwise would do for the benefit of their families, it is determined that no payment shall be made for improved lands over and above one eighth part of the tract allowed and reserved for such person to live on and occupy.

Art. 6. The Chickasaw Nation cannot receive any part of the payment for their land until it shall be surveyed and sold; therefore, in order to the greater facility in surveying and preparing the land for sale, and for keeping the business of the Nation separate and apart from the business and accounts of the United States, it is proposed by the Chickasaws, and agreed to, that a Surveyor General be appointed by the President to superintend alone the surveying of this ceded country, or so much thereof as the President may direct, who shall appoint a sufficient number of deputy surveyors as may be necessary to complete the survey in as short a time as may be reasonable and expedient. That the said Surveyor General be allowed one good clerk and one good draftsman to aid and assist him in the business of his office in preparing the lands for sale. It is also agreed that one land office be established for the sale of the lands, to have one register and one receiver of moneys, to be appointed by the President, and each register and receiver to have one good clerk to aid and assist them in the duties of their office. The surveyor's office, and the office of the register and receiver of money, shall be kept somewhere central in the Nation, at such place as the President of the United States may direct. As the before-mentioned officers and clerks are to be employed entirely in business of the Nation, appertaining to preparing and selling the land, they will, of course, be paid out of the proceeds of the sales of the ceded lands. That the Chickasaws may now understand, as near as may be, the expenses that will be incurred in the transacting of this business, it is proposed and agreed to, that the salary of the surveyor general be fifteen hundred dollars a year, and that the register and receiver of moneys be allowed twelve hundred dollars a year each, as a full compensation for their services, and all expenses, except stationery, and postages on their official business; and that each of the clerks and draftsmen be allowed seven hundred and fifty dollars a year for their services and all expenses.

Art. 7. It is expressly agreed that the United States shall not grant any right of preference to any person, or right of occupancy, in any manner whatsoever, but, in all cases of either public or private sale, they are to sell the land to the highest bidder; and also, that none of the lands be sold in smaller tracts than quarter sections or fractional sections of the same size, as near as may be, until the Chickasaw Nation may require the President to sell in smaller tracts. The chiefs of the Nation have heard that at some of the sales of the United States lands, the people there present entered into combinations, and united in purchasing much of the land at reduced prices for their own benefit, to the great prejudice of the government, and they express fears that attempts will be made to cheat them in the same manner when their lands shall be offered at public auction: It is therefore agreed that the President will use his best endeavors to prevent such combinations, or any other plan or state of things which may tend to prevent the land selling for its full value.

Art. 8. As the Chickasaws have determined to sell their country, it is desirable that the Nation realize the greatest possible sum for their lands which can be obtained; it is therefore proposed and agreed to, that after the President shall have offered their lands for sale, and shall have sold all that will sell for the government price, then the price shall be reduced so as to induce purchasers to buy who would not take the land at the government minimum price; and it is believed that five years from and after the date of the first sale will dispose of all the lands that will sell at the government price. If, then, at the expiration of five years, as before mentioned, the Chickasaw Nation may request the President to sell at such reduced price as the Nation may then propose, it shall be the duty of the President to comply with their request, by first offering it at public and afterwards at private sale, as in all other cases of selling public lands.

ART. 9. The Chickasaw Nation express their ignorance and incapacity to live and be happy under the State laws; they cannot read and understand them, and, therefore, they will always need a friend to advise and direct them; and fearing at some day the government of the United States may withdraw from them the agent under whose instructions they have lived so long and happy, they therefore request that the agent may be continued with him while here, and wherever they may remove to and settle. It is the earnest wish of the United States Government to see the Chickasaw Nation prosper and be happy, and, so far as is consistent, they will contribute all in their power to render them so; therefore, their request is granted. There shall be an agent kept with the Chickasaws as heretofore, so long as they live within the jurisdiction of the United States as a Nation, either within the limits of the States, where they now reside, or at any other place; and whenever the office of agent shall be vacant, and an agent to be appointed, the President will pay due respect to the wishes of the Nation, in selecting a man in all respects qualified to discharge the responsible duties of that office.

ART. 10. Whenever the Chickasaw Nation shall determine to remove from and leave their present country, they will give the President of the United States timely notice of such intention, and the President will furnish them the necessary funds and means for their transportation and journey, and for one year's provisions after they reach their new homes, in such quantity as the Nation may require; and the full amount of such funds, transportation and provisions is to be paid for out of the proceeds of the sales of the ceded lands. And should the Chickasaw Nation remove from their present country before they receive money from the sale of the lands hereby ceded, then and in that case the United States shall furnish them any reasonable sum of money for National purposes which may be deemed proper by the President of the United States; which sum shall also be refunded out of the sales of the ceded lands.

Art. 11. The Chickasaw Nation have determined to create a perpetual fund, for the use of the Nation for ever, out of the proceeds of the country now ceded away; and for that purpose they propose to invest a large proportion of the money arising from the sale of the land in some safe and valuable stocks, which will bring them in an annual interest or dividend, to be used for all National purposes, leaving the principal untouched, intending to use the interest alone. It is therefore proposed by the Chickasaws and agreed to, that the sum to be laid out in stocks as abovementioned shall be left with the Government of the United States until it can be laid out under the direction of the President of the United States, by and with the advice and consent of the Senate, in such safe and valuable stock as he may approve of, for the use and benefit of the Chickasaw Nation. The sum thus to be invested shall be equal to at least three-fourths of the whole nett proceeds of the sales of the lands, and as much more as the Nation may determine, if there shall be a surplus after supplying all the National wants. But it is hereby provided, that if the reasonable wants of the Nation shall require more than one-fourth of the proceeds of the sales of the land, then they may, by the consent of the President and Senate, draw from the Government such sum as may be thought reasonable, for valuable National purposes, out of the three-fourths reserved to be laid out in stocks. But if any of the moneys shall be thus drawn out of the sum first proposed to be laid out on interest, the sum shall be replaced out of the first moneys of the Nation which may come into the possession of the United States Government from the sale of the ceded lands, over and above the reasonable wants of the Nation. At the expiration of fifty years from this date, if the Chickasaw Nation shall have improved in education and civilization, and become so enlightened as to be capable of managing so large a sum of money to advantage, and with safety for the benefit of the Nation, and the President of the United States, with the Senate, shall be satisfied thereof, at that time, and shall give their consent thereto, the Chickasaw Nation may then withdraw the whole or any part of the fund now set apart to be laid out in stocks or at interest, and dispose of the same in any manner that they may think proper at that time for the use and benefit of the whole Nation; but no part of said fund shall ever be used for any other purpose than the benefit of the whole Chickasaw Nation. In order to facilitate the survey and sale of the lands now ceded, and to raise the money therefrom as soon as possible for the foregoing purpose, the President of the United States is authorized to commence the survey of the land as soon as may be practicable after the ratification of this treaty.

Art. 12. The Chickasaws feel grateful to their old chiefs for their long and faithful services, in attending to the business of the Nation; they believe it a duty to keep them from want in their old and declining age; with these feelings they have looked upon their old and beloved chief Tish-o-mingo, who is now grown old, and is poor and not able to live in that comfort which his valuable life and great merit deserve. It is therefore determined to give him, out of the National funds, one hundred dollars a year during the balance of his life, and the Nation request him to receive it as a token of their kind feelings for him, on account of his long and valuable services. Our old and beloved Queen, Puc-caun-la, is now very old and very poor. Justice, says the Nation, ought not to let her suffer in her old age; it is therefore determined to give her, out of the National funds, fifty dollars a year during her life, the money to be put in the hands of the agent to be laid out for her support, under his directions, with the advice of the chiefs.

Art. 13. The boundary line between the lands of the Chickasaws and Choctaws has never been run or properly defined; and as the Choctaws have sold their country to the United States, they now have no interest in the decision of that question. It is therefore agreed to call on the old Choctaw chiefs, to determine the line to be run between the Chickasaws and their former country. The Chickasaws by a reaty made with the United States at Franklin, in Tennessee, in August, 1830, declared their line to run as follows, to wit: Beginning at the mouth of the Oak-tibby-haw and running up said stream to a point, being a marked tree, on the old Natches road, one mile southwardly from Wall's old place; thence with the Choctaw boundary and along it westwardly through the Tunica old fields, to a point on the Mississippi river about twenty-eight miles by water, below where the St. Francis river enters said stream on the west side. It is now agreed that the surveys of the Choctaw country which are now in progress shall not cross the line until the true line shall be decided and determined, which shall be done as follows: the agent of the Choctaws on the west side of the Mississippi shall call on the old and intelligent chiefs of that Nation, and lay before them the line as claimed by the Chickasaws at the Franklin treaty; and if the Choctaws shall determine that line to be correct, then it shall be established and made the permanent line; but if the Choctaws say the line strikes the Mississippi river higher up said stream, then the evidence which can be had from both Nations shall be taken by the agents of both Nations and submitted to the President of the United States for his decision; and on such evidence the President will determine the true line on principles of strict justice.

Art. 14. As soon as the surveys are made, it shall be the duty of the chiefs, with the advice and assistance of the agent, to cause a correct list to be made out of all and every tract of land which shall be reserved for the use and benefit of the Chickasaw people, for their residence, as is provided for in the fourth article of this treaty; which list will designate the sections of land which are set apart for each family or individual in the Nation, showing the precise tracts which shall belong to each and every one of them; which list shall be returned to the register of the land office, and he shall make a record of the same in his office, to prevent him from offering any of said tracts of land for sale, and also as evidence of each person's lands. All the residue of the lands will be offered by the President for sale.

ART. 15. The Chickasaws request that no person be permitted to move in and settle on their country before the land is sold. It is therefore agreed, that no person whatsoever, who is not Chickasaw, or connected with the Chickasaws by marriage, shall be permitted to come into the country and settle on any part of the ceded lands until they shall be offered for sale, and then there shall not be any person permitted to settle on any of the land which has not been sold at the time of such settlement; and in all cases of a person settling on any of the ceded lands contrary to this express understanding, they will be intruders, and must be treated as such, and put off of the lands of the Nation.

In witness of all and every thing herein determined between the United States and the whole of the Chickasaw Nation in general council assembled, the parties have hereunto set their hands and seals, at the council-house, on Pontitock Creek, in the Chickasaw Nation, on the twentieth day of October, one thousand eight hundred and thirty-two.

JOHN COFFEE,		(L. S.)
ISH-TE-HO-TO-PA, (King,)	his × mark,	(L. S.)
TISH-O-MINGO,	his × mark,	(L. S.)
LEVI COLBERT,	his × mark,	(L. S.)
GEORGE COLBERT,	his × mark,	(L. S.)
WILLIAM McGILVERY,	his × mark,	(L. S.)
SAMUEL SELY,	his × mark,	(L. S.)
TO-PUL-KAH,	his × mark,	(L. S.)
ISAAC ALBERTSON,	his × mark,	(L. S.)
EM-UB-BY,	his × mark,	(L. S.)
PIS-TAH-LAH-TUBBE,	his × mark,	(L. S.)
ISH-TIM-O-LUT-KA,	his × mark,	(L. S.)
JAMES BROWN,	his × mark,	(L. S.)
IM-MAH-LOO-LO-TUBBE,	his × mark,	(L. S.)
ISH-TA-HA-CHAH,	his × mark,	(L. S.)
LAH-FIN-HUBBE,	his × mark,	(L. S.)
SHOP-POW-ME,	his × mark,	(L. S.)
NIN-UCK-AH-UMBA,	his × mark,	(L. S.)
IM-MAH-HOO-LA-TUBBE,	his × mark,	(L. S.)
ILLUP-PAH-UMBA,	his × mark,	(L. S.)

PITMAN COLBERT,		(L. S.)
CON-MUSH-KA-ISH-KAH,	his × mark,	(L. S.)
JAMES WOLFE,		(L. S.)
BAH-HA-KAH-TUBBE,	his × mark,	(L. S.)
E. BAH-KAH-TUBBE,	his × mark,	(L. S.)
CAPTAIN THOMPSON,	his × mark,	(L. S.)
NEW-BERRY,	his × mark,	(L. S.)
BAH-MA-HAH-TUBBE,	his × mark,	(L. S.)
JOHN LEWIS,	his × mark,	(L. S.)
I-YAH-HOU-TUBBE,	his × mark,	(L. S.)
TOK-HOLTH-LA-CHA,	his × mark,	(L. S.)
OKE-LAH-NAH-NUBBE,	his × mark,	(L. S.)
IM-ME-TUBBE,	his × mark,	(L. S.)
IN-KAH-YEA,	his × mark,	(L. S.)
AH-SHA-CUBBE,	his × mark,	(L. S.)
IM-MAH-HO-BAH,	his × mark,	(L. S.)
FIT-CHA-PLA,	his × mark,	(L. S.)
UNTE-MI-AH-TUBBE,	his × mark,	(L. S.)
OKE-LAH-HIN-LUBBE,	his × mark,	(L. S.)
JOHN GLOVER,	his × mark,	(L. S.)
BAH-ME-HUBBE,	his × mark,	(L. S.)
HUSH-TAH-TAH-UBBE,	his × mark,	(L. S.)
UN-TI-HA-KAH-TUBBE,	his × mark,	(L. S.)
YUM-MO-TUBBE,	his × mark,	(L. S.)
OH-HA-CUBBE,	his × mark,	(L. S.)
AH-FAH-MAH,	his × mark,	(L. S.)
AH-TA-KIN-TUBBE,	his × mark,	(L. S.)
AH-TO-KO-WAH,	his × mark,	(L. S.)
TAH-HA-CUBBE,	his × mark,	(L. S.)
KIN-HOI-CHA,	his × mark,	(L. S.)
ISH-TE-AH-TUBBE,	his × mark,	(L. S.)
CHIK-AH-SHA-NAN-UBBE,	his × mark,	(L. S.)
CHE-WUT-TA-HA,	his × mark,	(L. S.)
FO-LUT-TA-CHAH,	his × mark,	(L. S.)
NO-WO-KO,	his × mark,	(L. S.)
WIN-IN-A-PA,	his × mark,	(L. S.)
OKE-LAH-SHAH-CUBBE,	his × mark,	(L. S.)
ISH-TA-KI-YU-KA-TUBBE,	his × mark,	(L. S.)
MAH-TE-KO-SHUBBE,	his × mark,	(L. S.)
TOM-CHICK-AH,	his × mark,	(L. S.)

EI-O-CHE-TUBBE,	his × mark,	(L. S.)
NUCK-SHO-PUBBE,	his × mark,	(L. S.)
FAH-LAH-MO-TUBBE,	his × mark,	(L. S.)
CO-CHUB-BE,	his × mark,	(L. S.)
THOMAS SELY,	his × mark,	(L. S.)
OKE-LAH-SHA-PI-A,	his × mark,	(L. S.)

Signed and sealed in the presence of
BEN. REYNOLDS, Indian Agent.
JOHN L. ALLEN, Sub-Agent.
NATH. ANDERSON, Sec. to the Comm'r.
BENJ. LOVE, U. S. Interpreter.
ROBERT GORDON, Miss.
GEORGE WIGHTMAN, of Miss.
JOHN DONLEY, Tennessee.
D. S. PARRISH, Tennessee.
S. DAGGETT, Miss.
WM. A. CLURM.
G. W. LONG.

CHICKASAWS.

[CONCLUDED MAY 24, 1834. RATIFIED* JULY 1, 1834.]

ARTICLES OF CONVENTION AND AGREEMENT *proposed by the Commissioners, on the part of the United States, in pursuance of the request made by the Delegation representing the Chickasaw Nation of Indians, and which have been agreed to.*

ARTICLE 1. It is agreed that perpetual amity, peace and friendship shall exist between the United States and the Chickasaw Nation of Indians.

ART. 2. The Chickasaws are about to abandon their homes which they have long cherished and loved, and though

* With the exception of the third article in the supplementary articles.

hitherto unsuccessful, they still hope to find a country adequate to the wants and support of their people somewhere west of the Mississippi, and within the territorial limits of the United States. Should they do so, the Government of the United States hereby consent to protect and defend them against the inroads of any other tribe of Indians, and from the whites, and agree to keep them without the limits of any State or Territory. The Chickasaws pledge themselves never to make war upon any Indian people, or upon the whites, unless they are so authorized by the United States; but if war be made upon them they will be permitted to defend themselves until assistance be given to them by the United States, as shall be the case.

ART. 3. The Chickasaws are not acquainted with the laws of the whites, which are extended over them; and the many intruders which break into their country, interrupting their rights and disturbing their repose, leave no alternative whereby restraint can be afforded other than an appeal to the military force of the country, which they are unwilling to ask for or see resorted to; and therefore they agree to forbear such a request, for the prevention of this great evil, with the understanding, which is admitted, that the agent of the United States, upon the application of the chiefs of the Nation, will resort to every legal civil remedy, (at the expense of the United States,) to prevent intrusions upon the ceded country; and to restrain and remove trespassers from any selected reservations, upon application of the owner of the same. And it is also agreed, that the United States will continue some discreet person as agent, such as they now have, to whom they can look for redress of wrongs and injuries which may be attempted against them; and it is consented, that if any of their property be taken by persons of the United States, covertly or forcibly, the agent, on satisfactory and just complaint being made, shall pursue all lawful civil means which the laws of the State permit in which the wrong is done to regain the same or to obtain a just remuneration; and on failure or inability to procure redress for the offended against the offending party, payment for the loss sustained, on production of the record and certificate of the facts by the agent, shall be made by the United States; but in all such cases satisfactory proof for the establishing of the claim shall be offered.

Art. 4. The Chickasaws desire to have within their own direction and control the means of taking care of themselves: many of their people are quite competent to manage their affairs, though some are not capable, and might be imposed upon by designing persons; [it] is therefore agreed that the reservations hereinafter admitted shall not be permitted to be sold, leased or disposed of, unless it appear by the certificate of at least two of the following persons, to wit: Ish-ta-ho-ta-pa the king, Levi Colbert, George Colbert, Martin Colbert, Isaac Albertson, Henry Love, and Benjamin Love, of which five have affixed their names to this treaty, that the party owning or claiming the same is capable to manage and to take care of his or her affairs, which fact, to the best of his knowledge and information, shall be certified by the agent; and, furthermore, that a fair consideration has been paid, and thereupon the deed of conveyance shall be valid, provided the President of the United States, or such other person as he may designate, shall approve of the same and endorse it on the deed, which said deed and approval shall be registered at the place, and within the time required by the laws of the State in which the land may be situated; otherwise to be void. And where such certificate is not obtained upon the recommendation of a majority of the delegation, and the approval of the agent, at the discretion of the President of the United States, the same may be sold; but the consideration thereof shall remain as a part of the general Chickasaw fund in the hands of the government, until such time as the chiefs in council shall think it advisable to pay to the claimant or to those who may rightfully claim under said claimant, and shall so recommend it. And as the king, Levi Colbert, and the delegation, who have signed this agreement, and to whom certain important and interesting duties pertaining to the Nation are assigned, may die, resign, or remove, so that the people may be without the benefit of their services, it is stipulated, that as often as any vacancy happens, by death, resignation, or otherwise, the chiefs shall select some discreet person of their Nation to fill the occurring vacancy, who, upon a certificate of qualification, discretion and capability, by the agent, shall be appointed by the Secretary of War ; whereupon he shall possess all the authority granted to those who are here named, and the Nation will make to the person so appointed such reasonable compensation as they, with the assent of the agent and the Secretary of War, may think right, proper and reasonable to be allowed.

ART. 5. It is agreed that the fourth article of the "Treaty of Pontitock" be so changed that the following reservations be granted in fee :—to heads of families, being Indians, or having Indian families consisting of ten persons and upwards, four sections of land are reserved. To those who have five and less than ten persons, three sections. To those who have less than five, two sections. Also, those who own more than ten slaves shall be entitled to an additional section ; and those owning ten and less than ten, to half a section. These reservations shall be confined to the sections or fractional sections on which the party claiming lives, or to such as are contiguous or adjoining to the sections resided upon, subject to the following restrictions and conditions:

Firstly—In cases where there are interferences arising, the oldest occupant or settler shall have the preference; or,

Secondly—Where the land is adjudged unfit for cultivation by the agent, and three of the seven persons named in the fourth article above, the party entitled shall be and is hereby authorized to locate his claim upon other lands which may be unappropriated, and not subject to any other claim; and where two or more persons insist upon the entry of the same unappropriated section or fractional section, the priority of right shall be determined by lot; and where a fractional section is taken, leaving a balance greater or less than the surveyed subdivision of a section, then the deficiency shall be made up by connecting all the deficiencies so arising; and the register and receiver thereupon shall locate full or fractional sections, fit for cultivation, in the names respectively of the different persons claiming, which shall be held by them as tenants in common, according to the respective interests of those who are concerned ; and the proceeds, when sold by the parties claiming, shall be divided according to the interests which each may have in said section, or fractional section so located, or the same may be divided agreeably to quality or quantity.

Art. 6. Also, reservations of a section to each shall be granted to persons, male and female, not being heads of families, who are of the age of twenty-one years and upwards, a list of whom, within a reasonable time, shall be made out by the seven persons hereinbefore mentioned, and filed with the agent, upon whose certificate of its believed accuracy the register and receiver shall caused said reservation to be located upon the lands fit for cultivation, but not to interfere with the settlement rights of others. The persons thus entitled are to be excluded from the estimated numbers contained in any family enumeration, as is provided for in the fifth article preceding; and as to the sale, lease, or disposition of their reserves, they are to be subject to the conditions and restrictions set forth in the fourth article. In these and all other reserves where the party owning or entitled shall die, the interest in the same shall belong to his wife, or the wife and children, or to the husband, or to the husband and children, if there be any; and in cases of death, where there is neither husband, wife, nor children left, the same shall be disposed of for the general benefit, and the proceeds go into the general Chickasaw fund. But where the estate, as is prescribed in this article, comes to the children, and having so come, either of them die, the survivor or survivors of them shall be entitled to the same. But this rule shall not endure longer than for five years, nor beyond the period when the Chickasaws may leave their present for a new home.

Art. 7. Where any white man, before the date hereof, has married an Indian woman, the reservation he may be entitled to under this treaty, she being alive, shall be in her name, and no right of alienation of the same shall pertain to the husband, unless he divest her of the title after the mode and manner that *femes covertes* usually divest themselves of title to real estate, that is, by the ackowledgement of the wife, which may be taken before the agent and certiified by him that she consents to the sale freely and without compulsion from her husband, who shall at the same time certify that the head of such family is prudent and competent to take care of and manage his affairs; otherwise the proceeds of said sale shall be subject to the provisions and restrictions contained in the fourth article of this agreement. Rights to reservations, as are herein and in other articles of this agreement secured, will pertain to those who have heretofore intermarried with the Chickasaws and are residents of the Nation.

Art. 8. Males and females below the age of twenty-one years whose father being dead and the mother again has married, or who have neither father nor mother, shall each be entitled to half a section of land, but shall not be computed as parts of families under the fifth article, the same to be located under the direction of the agent, and under the supervision of the Secretary of War, so as not to interfere with any settlement right. These lands may be sold upon a recommendation of a majority of the seven persons, heretofore named in this agreement, setting forth that it will prove advantageous to the parties interested; subject, however, to the approval of the President, or such other person as he shall designate. If sold, the funds arising shall be retained in the possession of the Government, or, if the President deem it advisable, they shall be invested in stocks for the benefit of the parties interested, if there be a sufficient sum to be invested, (and it can be invested,) until such person marry or come of age, when the amount shall be paid over to those who are entitled to receive it—provided a majority of the seven persons, with the agent, shall certify, that, in their opinion, it will be to their interest and advantage; then, and in that case, the proceeds shall be paid over to the party or parties entitled to receive them.

Art. 9. But, in running the sectional lines, in some cases it will happen at [that] the spring and the dwelling house, or the spring and the cleared land, or the cleared land and the dwelling house of the settlers may be separated by sectional lines, whereby manifest inconvenience and injury will be occasioned; it is agreed, that when any of these occurrences arise, the party shall be entitled, as parts and portions of his reservations, to the adjoining section or fraction, as the case may be, unless there be some older occupant claiming a preference; and, in that event, the right of the party shall extend no farther than to give the person thus affected and injured, so much of his separated property as will secure the spring; also, where a sectional line shall separate any improvement, dwelling house, kitchen or stable, so much of the section as contains them shall be added into the occupied section as will secure them to their original owner; and then, and in that case, the older occupant being deprived of preference, shall have his deficiency thus occasioned made up to him by some fractional sectional section, or after the mode pointed out in the latter part of the fifth article of this treaty.

Art. 10. Reservations will be admitted to the following persons in addition to those which may be claimed under the fifth article of this treaty, to wit: Four sections to their old and beloved chief, Levi Colbert; to George Colbert, Martin Colbert, Isaac Albertson, Henry Love, and Benj. Love, in consideration of the trouble they have had in coming to Washington, and the further trouble hereafter to be encountered in taking care of the interests of their people under the provisions of this treaty, one section of land to each. Also, there is a fractional section between the residence of George Colbert and the Tennessee river, upon which he has a ferry; it is therefore consented, that said George Colbert shall own and have so much of said fraction as may be contained in the following lines, to wit: Beginning near Smith's ferry, at the point where the base meridian line and the Tennessee river come in contact; thence south so far as to pass the dwelling house, (and sixty yards beyond it,) within which is interred the body of his wife; thence east to the river, and down to the same point of beginning. Also, there shall be reserved to him an island in said river, nearly opposite to this fraction, commonly called Colbert's Island. A reservation also of two sections is admitted to Ish-ta-ho-ta-pa, the king of the Chickasaw Nation. And to Min-ta-ho-yea, the mother of Charles Colbert, one section of land. Also, one section, each, to the following persons: Im-mub-bee, Ish-tim-o-lut-ka, Ah-to-ho-woh, Pis-tah-lah-tubbe, Capt. Samuel Seley, and William McGilvery. To Col. Benj. Reynolds, their long tried and faithful agent, who has guarded their interest and twice travelled with their people far west beyond the Mississippi, to aid them in seeking and finding a home, there is granted two sections of land. Jointly to William Cooper and James Davis, lawyers of Mississippi, who have been faithful to the Indians, in giving them professional advice and legal assistance, and who are to continue to do so, within the States of Tennessee, Alabama, and Mississippi, while the Chickasaw people remain in said States, one section is granted. To Mrs. Margaret Allen, wife of the sub-agent, in her own right, half a section. These reservations to Benj. Reynolds, William Cooper, James Davis, and Margaret Allen, are to be located so as not to interfere with the Indian reservations.

Art. 11. After the reservations are taken and located, which shall be the case as speedily as may be after the surveys are completed, of which the register and receiver shall give notice, the residue of the Chickasaw country shall be sold as public lands of the United States are sold, with this difference: the lands as surveyed shall be offered at public sale, at a price not less than one dollar and a quarter per acre; and thereafter, for one year, those which are unsold and which have been previously offered at public sale shall be liable to private entry and sale at that price; thereafter, and for one year after, they shall be subject to entry and private sale at one dollar per acre; thereafter, during the third year, they shall be subject to sale and entry at fifty cents per acre; thereafter, and during the fourth year, at twenty-five cents per acre; and afterwards at twelve and a half cents per acre. But it may happen in the fourth and after years that the expenses may prove greater than the receipts, it is agreed that at any time after the third year the Chickasaws may declare the residue of their lands abandoned to the United States, and if so, they shall be henceforth acquitted of all and every expense on account of the sale of the same.

And that they may be advised of these matters, it is stipulated that the Government of the United States, within six months after any public sale takes place, shall advise them of the receipts and expenditures and of balances in their favor; and also, at regular intervals of six months after the first report is made, will afford them information of the proceeds of all entries and sales. The funds thence resulting, after the necessary expenses of surveying and selling and other advances which may be made are repaid to the United States, shall from time to time be invested in some secure stocks, redeemable within a period of not more than twenty years; and the United States will cause the interest arising therefrom annually to be paid to the Chickasaws.

Art. 12. When any portion of the country is fully surveyed, the President may order the same to be sold, but will allow six months from the date of the first sale, and three months' notice of any subsequent intended public sale, within which periods of time those who can claim reservations in the offered ranges of the country, shall file their applications and entries with the register and receiver, that the name of the owner or claimant of the same may be entered and marked on the general plat, at the office, whereby mistakes in the sales may be avoided and injuries be prevented.

Art. 13. If the Chickasaws shall be so fortunate as to procure a home within the limits of the United States, it is agreed, that, with the consent of the President and Senate, so much of their invested stocks as may be necessary to the purchase of a country for them to settle in shall be permitted to them to be sold, or the United States will advance the necessary amount, upon a guarantee and pledge of an equal amount of their stocks; also, as much of them may be sold, with the consent of the President and Senate, as shall be adjudged necessary for establishing schools, mills, blacksmiths' shops; and for the education of their children; and for any other needful purpose which their situation and condition may make, and by the President and Senate be considered necessary; and on the happening of such a contingency, and information thereof being given of an intention of the whole or any portion of the nation to remove, the United States will furnish competent persons safely to conduct them to their future destination, and also supplies necessary to the same, and for one year after their arrival at the west, provided the Indians shall desire supplies to be furnished for so long a period; the supplies so afforded to be chargeable to the general Chickasaw account, provided the funds of said nation shall be found adequate to the expenses, which under this and other articles of this agreement may be required.

ART. 14. It is understood and agreed that articles twelve and thirteen of the "treaty of Pontitock," of the twentieth day of October, one thousand eight hundred and thirty-two, and which was concluded with Gen. John Coffee, shall be retained; all other articles of said treaty inconsistent in any respect with the provisions of this are declared to be revoked. Also so much of the supplemental treaty as relates to Colbert Moore; to the bond of James Colbert transferred to Robert Gordon; to the central position of the land office; to the establishment of mail routes through the Chickasaw country; and as it respects the privilege given to John Doneley, be and the same are declared to be in full force.

ART. 15. By the sixth article of a treaty made with the Chickasaw Nation, by Andrew Jackson and Isaac Shelby, on the nineteenth day of October, one thousand eight hundred and eighteen, it was provided that a commissioner should be appointed to mark the southern boundary of said cession; now it is agreed that the line which was run and marked by the commissioner on the part of the United States, in pursuance of said treaty, shall be considered the true line to the extent that the rights and interests of the Chickasaws are concerned, and no farther.

ART. 16. The United States agree that the appropriation made by Congress, in the year one thousand eight hundred and thirty-three, for carrying into effect "the treaty with the Chickasaws," shall be applicable to this, to be reimbursed by them; and their agent may receive and be charged with the same, from time to time, as, in the opinion of the Secretary of War, any portion may be wanted for national purposes by the Chickasaws; of which nature and character shall be considered their present visit to Washington city.

Done at the city of Washington, on the 24th day of May, one thousand eight hundred and thirty-four.

IN. H. EATON,
Commissioner on the part of the U. S.
GEORGE COLBERT, his × mark.
ISAAC ALBERTSON, his × mark.
MARTIN COLBERT, (L. S.)
HENRY LOVE, (L. S.)
BENJAMIN LOVE, (L. S.)

Witnesses:
CHARLES F. LITTLE, *Secretary to Commissioner.*
BEN. REYNOLDS, *Indian Agent.*
G. W. LONG.
JAMES STANDEFER.
THOMAS S. SMITH.
SAM'L SWARTWOUT,
WM. GORDON.
F. W. ARMSTRONG, *C. Agent.*
JOHN M. MILLARD.

The undersigned, appointed by the Chickasaw Nation of Indians, in the two-fold capacity of a delegate and interpreter, hereby declares that in all that is set forth in the above articles of convention and agreement, have been by him fully and accurately interpreted and explained, and that the same has been approved by the entire delegation.

May 24, 1834.

BENJAMIN LOVE, *Delegate and Interpreter.*

CHARLES F. LITTLE, *Secretary to Commissioner.*

BEN. REYNOLDS, *Ind. Agent.*

Articles supplementary to those concluded and signed by the United States Commissioner and the Chickasaw delegation, on the twenty-fourth day of May, one thousand eight hundred and thirty-four, which, being agreed to by the President and Senate of the United States, are to stand as part of said treaty.

ART. 1. It is represented that the old chiefs, Levi Colbert and Isaac Albertson, who having rendered many and valuable services to their nation, desire, on account of their health, to visit some watering place, during the present year, for recovery and restoration; it is agreed that there be paid to the agent for these purposes, and to discharge some debts which are due and owing from the nation, the sum of three thousand dollars, out of the appropriation of one thousand eight hundred and thirty-three, for carrying into effect the "treaty of Pontitock," which sum so far as used is to be hereafter reimbursed to the nation by said Levi Colbert and Isaac Albertson, and by the nation to the United States, as other advances are to be reimbursed from the sale of their lands.

ART. 2. The Chickasaw people express a desire that the Government shall, at the expense of the United States, educate some of their children, and they urge the justice of their application, on the ground that they have ever been faithful and friendly to the people of this country; that they have never raised the tomahawk to shed the blood of an American, and have given up heretofore to their white brothers extensive and valuable portions of their country, at a price wholly inconsiderable and inadequate; and from which the United States have derived great wealth and important advantages; therefore, with the advice and consent of the President and Senate of the United States, it is consented that three thousand dollars for fifteen years be appropriated and applied, under the direction of the Secretary of War, for the education and instruction within the United States, of such children, male and female, or either, as the seven persons named in the treaty to which this is a supplement, and their successors, with the approval of the agent, from time to time, may select and recommend.

ART. 3. The Chickasaw Nation desire to close finally all the business they have on the east side of the Mississippi, that their great father may be no more troubled with their complaints, and to this end they ask the Government to receive from them a tract of land of four miles square, heretofore reserved under the fourth article of their "treaty of 1818," and to pay them, within three months from the date of this arrangement, the government price of one dollar and a quarter per acre for said reserve; and accordingly the same is agreed to, provided a satisfactory relinquishment of title from the parties interested be filed with the Secretary of War previous to payment being made.

ART. 4. Benj. Reynolds, agent at the time of paying their last annuity, had stolen from him, by a negro slave of the Chickasaws, a box containing one thousand dollars; the chiefs of the Chickasaw people satisfied of the facts, and hence unwilling to receive the last amount from their agent, ask, and it is agreed, that the sum so stolen and lost shall be passed to the credit of their nation by the United States, to be drawn on hereafter for their national purposes.

ART. 5. The Chickasaw people are aware that one clerk is insufficient to the bringing of their lands early into the market; and rather than encounter the delay which must ensue, they prefer the increased expenses of an additional one. It is therefore stipulated that the President shall appoint another clerk, at the same annual compensation agreed upon by the "treaty of Pontitock," who shall be paid after the manner prescribed therein. But whenever the President shall be of opinion that the services of any officer employed under this treaty, for the sale of lands, can be dispensed with, he will, in justice to the Chickasaws, to save them from unnecessary expenses, discontinue the whole, or such as can be dispensed with.

Signed the 24th of May, 1834.

IN. H. EATON,
Commissioner on the part of the U. S.
GEORGE COLBERT, his × mark.
ISAAC ALBERTSON, his × mark.
MARTIN COLBERT, (L. S.)
HENRY LOVE, (L. S.)
BENJAMIN LOVE, (L. S.)

Witnesses:
CHARLES F. LITTLE, *Secretary to Commissioner.*
BEN. REYNOLDS, *Indian Agent.*
G. W. LONG.
JAMES STANDEFER.
THOMAS S. SMITH.
SAM'L SWARTWOUT.
WM. GORDON.
F. W. ARMSTRONG, *C. Agent.*
JOHN M. MILLARD.

CHOCTAWS AND CHICKASAWS.

[CONCLUDED JANUARY 17, 1837. RATIFIED MARCH 24, 1837.]

ARTICLES OF CONVENTION AND AGREEMENT *made on the seventeenth day of January, one thousand eight hundred and thirty-seven, between the undersigned Chiefs and Com-*

missioners, duly appointed and empowered by the Choctaw Tribe of Red People, and John McLish, Pitman Colbert, James Brown, and James Perry, Delegates of the Chickasaw Tribe of Indians, duly authorized by the Chiefs and head men of said People for that purpose, subject to the approval of the President and Senate of the United States.

ARTICLE 1. It is agreed by the Choctaws that the Chickasaws shall have the privilege of forming a district within the limits of their country, to be held on the same terms that the Choctaws now hold it, except the right of disposing of it, which is held in common with the Choctaws and Chickasaws, to be called the Chickasaw district of the Choctaw Nation, to have an equal representation in their General Council, and to be placed on an equal footing in every other respect with any of the other districts of said Nation, except a voice in the management of the consideration which is given for these rights and privileges; and the Chickasaw people to be entitled to all the rights and privileges of the Choctaws, with the exception of participating in the Choctaw annuities and the consideration to be paid for these rights and privileges, and to be subject to the same laws to which the Choctaws are; but the Chickasaws reserve to themselves the sole right and privilege of controlling and managing the residue of their funds, as far as is consistent with the late treaty between said people and the Government of the United States, and of making such regulations and selecting such officers for that purpose as they may think proper.

ART. 2. The Chickasaw district shall be bounded as follows, viz: beginning on the north bank of Red river, at the mouth of Island Bayou, about eight or ten miles below the mouth of False Wachitta, thence running north along the main channel of said bayou to its source; thence along the dividing ridge between the Wachitta and Low Blue rivers to the road leading from Fort Gibson to Fort Wachitta; thence along said road to the line dividing Mushalatubbee and Pushmatahaw districts; thence eastwardly along said district line to the source of Brushy creek; thence down said creek to where it flows into the Canadian river, ten or twelve miles above the mouth of the south fork of the Canadian; thence west along the main Canadian river to its source, if in the limits of the United States or to those limits, and thence due south to Red river and down Red river to the beginning.

ART. 3. The Chickasaws agree to pay the Choctaws, as a consideration for these rights and privileges, the sum of five hundred and thirty thousand dollars; thirty thousand of which shall be paid at the time and in the manner that the Choctaw annuity of 1837 is paid; and the remaining five hundred thousand dollars to be invested in some safe and secure stocks, under the direction of the Government of the United States, redeemable within a period of not less than twenty years; and the Government of the United States shall cause the interest arising therefrom to be paid annually to the Choctaws in the following manner: twenty thousand dollars of which to be paid as the present Choctaw annuity is paid, for four years, and the residue to be subject to the control of the General Council of the Choctaws; and, after the expiration of the four years, the whole of said interest to be subject to the entire control of the said council.

ART. 4. To provide for the future adjustment of all complaints or dissatisfactions which may arise to interrupt the peace and harmony which have so long and so happily existed between the Choctaws and Chickasaws, it is hereby agreed by the parties, that all questions relative to the construction of this agreement shall be referred to the Choctaw agent, to be by him decided; reserving, however, to either party, should it feel itself aggrieved thereby, the right of appealing to the President of the United States, whose decision shall be final and binding; but as considerable time might elapse before the decision of the President could be had, in the mean time the decision of the said agent shall be binding.

ART. 5. It is hereby declared to be the intention of the parties hereto, that equal rights and privileges shall pertain to both Choctaws and Chickasaws to settle in whatever district they may think proper, and to be eligible to all the different offices of the Choctaw Nation, and to vote on the same terms in whatever district they may settle, except that the Choctaws are not to vote in anywise for officers in relation to the residue of the Chickasaw fund.

In testimony whereof, the parties hereto have hereunto subscribed their names and affixed their seals, at Doaksville, near Fort Towson in the Choctaw country, on the day and year first above written.

In the presence of

WILLIAM ARMSTRONG,
Acting Superintendent Western Territory.

HENRY R. CARTER,
Cond'r of the Chickasaw Delegation.

JOSIAH S. DOAK,

VINCENT B. TIMS,

DANIEL McCURTAIN, *U. S. Interpreter.*

P. J. HUMPHEYS,

J. T. SPRAGUE, *Lieut. U. S. Marine Corps.*

THOMAS LAFLOOR, (his × mark,)
Chief of Oaklafalaya District.

NETUCHACHUE, (his × mark,)
Chief of Pushmalahaw District.

JOSEPH KINCAID, (his × mark,)
Chief of Mushalatubbee District.

Commissioners of the Choctaw Nation.

P. P. PITCHLYNN, (L. S.)

GEORGE W. HASKINS, (L. S.)

ISRAEL FOLSOM, (L. S.)

R. M. JONES, (L. S.)

SILAS D. FISHER, (L. S.)

SAMUEL WOWSTER, (L. S.)

JOHN McKENNEY, (his × mark,)

EYACHAHOFNA, (his × mark,)

NATHANIEL FOLSOM, (his × mark,)

LEWIS BRASHEARS, (his × mark,)
JAMES FLETCHER, (his × mark,)
GEORGE PUSLEY, (his × mark.)

Captains.

OAK-CHI-A, (his × mark,)
THOMAS HAYS, (his × mark,)
PIS-TAM-BEE, (his × mark,)
HO-LAH-TA-HO-MA, (his × mark,)
E-YO-TAH, (his × mark,)
ISAAC PERRY, (his × mark,)
NO-WAH-HAM-BEE, (his × mark.)

Chickasaw Delegation.

J. McLISH,
PITMAN COLBERT,
JAMES BROWN, (his × mark,)
JAMES PERRY, (his × mark.)

MILLARD FILLMORE,

PRESIDENT OF THE UNITED STATES OF AMERICA,

To all and singular to whom these presents shall come, Greeting:

Whereas, a treaty was made and concluded at the city of Washington, on the 22d day of June, 1852, between Kenton Harper, Commissioner on the part of the United States, and Colonel Edmund Pickens, Benjamin S. Love, and Sampson Folsom, Commissioners duly appointed for that purpose by the Chickasaw Tribe of Indians, which treaty is in the words and figures following, to wit:

ARTICLES OF A TREATY concluded at Washington on the 22d day of June, 1852, between Kenton Harper, Commissioner on the [part of the] United States, and Colonel Edmund

Pickens, Benjamin S. Love, and Sampson Folsom, Commissioners duly appointed for that purpose by the Chickasaw Tribe of Indians.

ART. 1. The Chickasaw Tribe of Indians acknowledge themselves to be under the guardianship of the United States, and as a means of securing the protection guarantied to them by former treaties, it is agreed that an agent of the United States shall continue to reside among them.

ART. 2. The expenses attending the sale of the lands ceded by the Chickasaws to the United States, under the treaty of 1852, having for some time past exceeded the receipts, it is agreed that the remnant of the lands so ceded, and yet unsold, shall be disposed of as soon as practicable, under the direction of the United States, in such manner and in such quantities as in his judgment shall be least expensive to the Chickasaws, and most conducive to their benefit; provided, that a tract of land including the graveyard near the town of Pontotoc, where many of the Chickasaws and their white friends are buried, and not exceeding four acres in quantity, shall be and is hereby set apart and conveyed to the said town of Pontotoc, to be held sacred for the purpose of a public burial ground forever.

ART. 3. It is hereby agreed that the question of right of the Chickasaws, so long contended for by them, to a reservation of four miles square on the river Sandy, in the State of Tennessee, and particularly described in the 4th article of the treaty concluded at Oldtown, on the 19th day of October, 1818, shall be submitted to the Secretary of the Interior, who shall decide what amount, if anything, shall be paid to the Chickasaws for said reservation; provided, however, that the amount so to be paid shall not exceed one dollar and twenty-five cents per acre.

ART. 4. The Chickasaws allege that, in the management and disbursement of their funds by the Government, they have been subjected to losses and expenses which properly should be borne by the United States. With the view, therefore, of doing justice in the premises, it is hereby agreed that there shall be, at as early a day as practicable, an account stated under the direction of the Secretary of the Interior, exhibiting in detail all the moneys which from time to time have been placed in the Treasury, to the credit of the Chickasaw Nation, resulting from the treaties of 1832 and 1834, and all the disbursements made therefrom ; and said account, as stated, shall be submitted to the Chickasaws, who shall have the privilege, within a reasonable time, of filing exceptions thereto, and any exceptions so filed shall be referred to the Secretary of the Interior, who shall adjudicate the same according to the principles of law and equity, and his decision shall be final and conclusive on all concerned.

It is also alleged by the Chickasaws, that there are numerous cases in which moneys held in trust by the United States for the benefit of orphan and incompetent Chickasaws, have been wrongfully paid out to persons having no right to receive the same.

It is therefore further agreed, that all such cases shall be investigated by the agent of the United State, under the direction of the Secretary of the Interior. And if it shall appear to the satisfaction of said Secretary, that any of the orphans and incompetents have been defrauded by such wrongful payment, the amount thus misapplied shall be accounted for by the United States as if no such payment had been made.

Art. 5. The Chickasaws are desirous that the whole amount of their National fund shall remain with the United States, in trust, for the benefit of their people, and that the same shall on no account be diminished.

It is therefore agreed that the United States shall continue to hold said fund in trust, as aforesaid, and shall constantly keep the same invested in safe and profitable stocks, the interest upon which shall be annually paid to the Chickasaw Nation ; provided, that so much of said fund as the Chickasaws may require for the purpose of enabling them to effect the permanent settlement of their Tribe, as contemplated by the treaty of 1834, shall be subject to the control of their General Council.

Art. 6. The powers and duties conferred on certain persons, particularly mentioned in the 4th article of the treaty of 1834, and their successors in office, shall hereafter be vested in and performed by the General Council of the Chickasaws, or such officers as may be by said council appointed for that purpose; and no certificate or deed given or executed by the persons aforesaid, from which the approval of the President of the United States has once been withheld, shall be hereafter approved unless the same shall first receive the sanction of the Chickasaw Council, or the officers appointed as aforesaid, and of the agent of the United States for said Chickasaw Nation.

Art. 7. No claim or account shall hereafter be paid by the Government of the United States out of the Chickasaw fund, unless the same shall have first been considered and allowed by the Chickasaw General Council; provided, however, that this clause shall not affect payments upon claims under existing contracts, made by the authority of the Chickasaw General Council, or interfere with the due administration of the Acts of Congress regulating trade and intercourse with the Indian tribes.

Art. 8. It is further agreed, that regular semi-annual accounts of the receipts and disbursements of the Chickasaw fund shall be furnished the Chickasaw Council by the Government of the United States.

Art. 9. The sum of fifteen hundred dollars shall be paid the Chickasaw Nation, in full of all expenses incurred by their Commissioners in negotiating this treaty.

In witness thereof, the contracting parties have hereunto set their hands and seals, the day and year above written.

KENTON HARPER, [SEAL.]
Commissioner for United States.

EDMUND PICKENS, his × mark, [SEAL.]
BENJAMIN S. LOVE, [SEAL.]
SAMPSOM FOLSOM, [SEAL.]
Commissioners for the Chickasaws.

In presence of—

CHARLES E. MIX, *Chief Clerk, Office Indian Affairs.*
L. R. SMOOT.
F. R. CRUTTENDEN.
H. MILLER.
AARON V. BROWN, *Interpreter.*

And whereas, the said treaty having been to the Senate of the United States, for its constitutional action thereon, the Senate did, on the thirteenth day of August, one thousand eight hundred and fifty-two, amend the same by a resolution in the words and figures following, to wit:

In Executive Session, Senate of the United States,
August 13th, 1852.

Resolved, (two-thirds of the Senators present concurring,) That the Senate advise and consent to the ratification of the articles of a treaty concluded at Washington on the 22d day of June, eighteen hundred and fifty-two, between Kenton Harper, Commissioner on the part of the United States, and Colonel Edmund Pickens, Benjamin S. Love, and Sampson Folsom, Commissioners duly appointed for that purpose by the Chickasaw tribe of Indians, with the following

Amendments.

At the end of the fourth article add the following:

Provided, That the provisions of this article shall not be so construed as to impose any obligation on the United States to reimburse any expenditures heretofore made in conformity with the stipulations contained in the treaties of 1832 and 1834; and provided, further, that the United States shall not be liable to repay moneys held in trust for the benefit of orphan and incompetent Chickasaws, in any case in which payment of such moneys has been made upon the recommendation or certificate of the persons appointed for that purpose in the fourth article of the treaty of 1834, or of their successors, and in other respects in conformity with the provisions of that article; and provided further, that the United States shall not be held responsible for any reservation of land, or of any sale, lease, or other disposition of the same, made, sold, leased, or otherwise disposed of in conformity with the several provisions of said treaties of 1832 and 1834.

After article nine, add the following new article:

Art. 10. And it is further stipulated that in no case hereafter shall any money due or to be paid under this treaty, or any former treaty between the same contracting parties, be paid to any agent or attorney; but shall in all cases be paid directly to the party or parties primarily entitled thereto.

Attest: ASBURY DICKENS, *Secretary.*

And whereas, the said amendments have been submitted and explained to the Chickasaw Indians in council assembled, the said Chickasaws did, on the sixteenth day of October, one thousand eight hundred and fifty-two, assent to said treaty as amended by the Senate, in words following, to wit:

Whereas, by an act of the General Council of the Chickasaws, passed 7th February, 1852, Col. Edmund Pickens, Benjamin S. Love, and Sampson Folsom, were appointed Commissioners on behalf of the Chickasaw people to negotiate a treaty with the United States, and the said Commissioners having on the 22d June, 1852, concluded a treaty with Kenton Harper, Commissioner on the part of the United States, and the said treaty having been ratified on the 13th August, 1852, by the Senate of the United States with certain amendments thereto, and said amendments having been duly considered and fully understood by the Council: Therefore, Be it enacted by the Chickasaws, in Council assembled, that the said Chickasaws do consent to and ratify said amendments, and hereby make the same as binding on the Chickasaw people as though the same had been a part of the original treaty.

Approved by the Council unanimously, October 16, 1852.

JAMES N. McLISH, *President of Council.*
DOUGHERTY COLBERT, *F. C.*

Attest:
H. Colbert, *Secretary.*

CHICKASAW AGENCY, Dec. 25, 1852.

I hereby certify that the foregoing Act of the Council, ratifying certain amendments to a treaty concluded at Washington on the 22d June, 1852, has been officially communicated to me by D. Colbert, financial chief of the Chickasaws, as an act passed by the Chickasaw Council, and that the same is authentic.

Given under my hand the day and year above written.

A. J. SMITH, *Chickasaw Agent.*

—

Now, therefore, be it known that I, Millard Fillmore, President of the United States of America, do, in pursuance of the advice and consent of the Senate, as expressed in their resolution of the thirteenth day of August, one thousand eight hundred and fifty-two, accept, ratify and confirm the said treaty as amended.

In testimony whereof, I have caused the seal of the United States to be affixed, having signed the same with my hand.

[L. S.] Done at the city of Washington, this twenty-fourth day of February, in the year of our Lord one thousand eight hundred and fifty-three, and of the Independence of the United States the seventy-seventh.

By the President, (Signed) MILLARD FILLMORE.
(Signed,) EDWARD EVERETT,
Secretary of State.

TREATY BETWEEN THE UNITED STATES AND THE CHOCTAW AND CHICKASAW INDIANS.

FRANKLIN PIERCE,

PRESIDENT OF THE UNITED STATES OF AMERICA,

To all and singular to whom these presents shall come, Greeting:

Whereas a treaty was made and concluded at the city of Washington, on the twenty-second day of June, one thousand eight hundred and fifty-five, by George W. Mannypenny, Commissioner on the part of the United States, Peter P. Pitchlynn, Israel Folsom, Samuel Garland, and Dixon W. Lewis, Commissioners on the part of the Choctaws, and Edmund Pickens and Sampson Folsom, Commissioners on the part of the Chickasaws, which treaty is in the words following, to wit:

"ARTICLES OF AGREEMENT AND CONVENTION *between the United States and the Choctaw and Chickasaw tribes of Indians, made and concluded at the city of Washington, the twenty-second day of June, A. D. one thousand eight hundred and fifty-five, by George W. Manypenny, Commissioner on the part of the United States; Peter P. Pitchlynn, Israel Folsom, Samuel Garland, and Dixon W. Lewis, Commissioners on the part of the Choctaws; and Edmund Pickens and Sampson Folsom, Commissioners on the part of the Chickasaws.*

"Whereas, the political connexion heretofore existing between the Choctaw and the Chickasaw tribes of Indians has given rise to unhappy and injurious dissensions and controversies among them, which render necessary a readjustment of their relations to each other and to the United States: and whereas, the United States desire that the Choctaw Indians shall relinquish all claim to any territory west of the one hundredth degree of west longitude, and, also, to make provision for the permanent settlement within the Choctaw country, of the Wichita and certain other tribes or bands of Indians, for which purpose the Choctaws and Chickasaws are willing to lease, on reasonable terms, to the United States, that portion of their common territory which is west of the ninety-eighth degree of west longitude: and whereas, the Choctaws contend that, by a just and fair construction of the treaty of September 27, 1830, they are, of right, entitled to the nett proceeds of the lands ceded by them to the United States under said treaty, and have proposed that the question of their right to the same, together with the whole subject-matter of their unsettled claims, whether national or individual, against the United States, arising under the various provisions of said treaty, shall be referred to the Senate of the United States for final adjudication and adjustment: and whereas, it is necessary for the simplification and better understanding of the relations between the United States and the Choctaw Indians, that all their subsisting treaty stipulations be embodied in one comprehensive instrument:

"Now, therefore, the United States of America, by their Commissioner, George W. Manypenny, the Choctaws, by their Commissioners, Peter P. Pitchlynn, Israel Folsom, Samuel Garland, and Dickson W. Lewis, and the Chickasaws, by their Commissioners, Edmund Pickens and Sampson Folsom, do hereby agree and stipulate as follows, viz:

"ARTICLE I. The following shall constitute and remain the boundaries of the Choctaw and Chickasaw country, viz: Beginning at a point on the Arkansas river, one hundred paces east of old Fort Smith, where the western boundary line of the State of Arkansas crosses the said river, and running thence due south to Red river; thence up Red river to the point where the meridian of one hundred degrees west longitude crosses the same; thence north along said meridian to the main Canadian river; thence down said river to its junction with the Arkansas river; thence down said river to the place of beginning.

"And pursuant to an act of Congress approved May 28, 1830, the United States do hereby forever secure and guaranty the lands embraced within the said limits to the members of the Choctaw and Chickasaw tribes, their heirs and successors, to be held in common; so that each and every member of either tribe shall have an equal, undivided interest in the whole: *Provided, however*, no part thereof shall ever be sold without the consent of both tribes; and that said land shall revert to the United States if said Indians and their heirs become extinct, or abandon the same.

"ARTICLE II. A district for the Chickasaws is hereby established, bounded as follows, to wit: beginning on the north bank of Red river, at the mouth of Island Bayou, where it empties into Red river, about twenty-six miles on a straight line, below the mouth of False Wachitta; thence running a northwesterly course along the main channel of said bayou, to the junction of the three prongs of said bayou, nearest the dividing ridge between Wachitta and Low Blue rivers, as laid down on Capt. R. L. Hunter's map; thence northerly along the eastern prong of Island Bayou to its source; thence due north to the Canadian river; thence west along the main Canadian to the ninety-eighth degree of west longitude; thence south to Red river; and thence down Red river to the beginning: *Provided, however*, if the line running due north, from the eastern source of Island Bayou, to the main Canadian, shall not include Allen's or Wa-pa-nacka academy, within the Chickasaw district, then an offset shall be made from said line, so as to leave said academy two miles within the Chickasaw district, north, west and south from the lines of boundary.

"ARTICLE III. The remainder of the country held in common by the Choctaws and Chickasaws shall constitute the Choctaw district, and their officers and people shall at all times have the right of safe conduct and free passage through the Chickasaw district.

"ARTICLE IV. The government and laws now in operation, and not incompatible with this instrument, shall be and remain in full force and effect within the limits of the Chickasaw district, until the Chickasaws shall adopt a constitution, and enact laws, superseding, abrogating, or changing the same. And all judicial proceedings within said district, commencing prior to the adoption of a constitution and laws by the Chickasaws, shall be conducted and determined according to existing laws.

"ARTICLE V. The members of either the Choctaw or the Chickasaw tribe shall have the right, freely, to settle within the jurisdiction of the other, and shall thereupon be entitled to all the rights, privileges, and immunities of citizens thereof; but no member of either tribe shall be entitled to participate in the funds belonging to the other tribe. Citizens of both tribes shall have the right to institute and prosecute suits in the courts of either, under such regulations as may from time to time be prescribed by their respective legislatures.

"Article VI. Any person duly charged with a criminal offence against the laws of either the Choctaw or the Chickasaw tribe, and escaping into the jurisdiction of the other, shall be promptly surrendered upon the demand of the proper authorities of the tribe within whose jurisdiction the offence shall be alleged to have been committed.

"Article VII. So far as may be compatible with the constitution of the United States and the laws made in pursuance thereof regulating trade and intercourse with the Indian tribes, the Choctaws and Chickasaws shall be secured in the unrestricted right of self-government, and full jurisdiction over persons and property within their respective limits; excepting, however, all persons with their property who are not by birth, adoption, or otherwise, citizens or members of either the Choctaw or Chickasaw tribe; and all persons, not being citizens or members of either tribe, found within their limits, shall be considered intruders, and be removed from and kept out of the same by the United States agent, assisted if necessary by the military, with the following exceptions, viz: Such individuals as are now, or may be in the employment of the government, and their families; those peacefully travelling or temporarily sojourning in the country or trading therein, under license from the proper authority of the United States, and such as may be permitted by the Choctaws or Chickasaws, with the assent of the United States agent, to reside within their limits, without becoming citizens or members of either of said tribes.

"Article VIII. In consideration of the foregoing stipulations, and immediately upon the ratification of this convention, there shall be paid to the Choctaws, in such manner as their National Council shall direct, out of the National fund of the Chickasaws held in trust by the United States, the sum of one hundred and fifty thousand dollars.

"ARTICLE IX. The Choctaw Indians do hereby absolutely and for ever quit-claim and relinquish to the United States all their right, title and interest in and to any and all lands west of the one hundredth degree of west longitude; and the Choctaws and Chickasaws do hereby lease to the United States all that portion of their common territory west of the ninety-eighth degree of west longitude, for the permanent settlement of the Wichita and such other tribes or bands of Indians as the government may desire to locate therein; excluding, however, all the Indians of New Mexico, and also those whose usual ranges at present are north of the Arkansas river, and whose permanent locations are north of the Canadian river, but including those bands whose permanent ranges are south of the Canadian or between it and the Arkansas; which Indians shall be subject to the exclusive control of the United States, under such rules and regulations, not inconsistent with the rights and interests of the Choctaws and Chickasaws, as may from time to time be prescribed by the President for their government: *provided, however*, the territory so leased shall remain open to settlement by Choctaws and Chickasaws as heretofore.

"ARTICLE X. In consideration of the foregoing relinquishment and lease, and as soon as practicable after the ratification of this convention, the United States will pay to the Choctaws the sum of six hundred thousand dollars, and to the Chickasaws the sum of two hundred thousand dollars, in such manner as their general councils shall respectively direct.

"ARTICLE XI. The government of the United States not being prepared to assent to the claim set up under the treaty of September the twenty-seventh, eighteen hundred and thirty, and so earnestly contended for by the Choctaws as a rule of settlement, but justly appreciating the sacrifices, faithful services and general good conduct of the Choctaw people, and being desirous that their rights and claims against the United States shall receive a just, fair and liberal consideration, it is therefore stipulated that the following questions be submitted for adjudication to the Senate of the United States:

"*First*—Whether the Choctaws are entitled to, or shall be allowed the proceeds of the sale of the lands ceded by them to the United States by the treaty of September the twenty-seventh, eighteen hundred and thirty, deducting therefrom the cost of their survey and sale, and all just and proper expenditures and payments under the provisions of said treaty; and if so, what price per acre shall be allowed to the Choctaws to the lands remaining unsold, in order that a final settlement with them may be promptly effected. Or,

"*Second*—Whether the Choctaws shall be allowed a gross sum in further and full satisfaction of all their claims, national and individual, against the United States; and if so, how much.

"ARTICLE XII. In case the Senate shall award to the Choctaws the nett proceeds of the lands ceded as aforesaid, the same shall be received by them in full satisfaction of all their claims against the United States, whether national or individual, arising under any former treaty; and the Choctaws shall thereupon become liable and bound to pay all such individual claims as may be adjudged by the proper authorities of the tribe to be equitable and just—the settlement and payment to be made with the advice and under the direction of the United States agent for the tribe; and so much of the fund, awarded by the Senate to the Choctaws as the proper authorities thereof shall ascertain and determine to be necessary for the payment of the just liabilities of the tribe, shall on their requisition be paid over to them by the United States. But should the Senate allow a gross sum in further and full satisfaction of all their claims, whether national or individual, against the United States, the same shall be accepted by the Choctaws, and they shall thereupon become liable for and bound to pay all the individual claims as aforesaid; it being expressly understood that the adjudication and decision of the Senate shall be final.

"Article XIII. The amounts secured by existing treaty stipulations—viz: permanent annuity of three thousand dollars, under the second article of the treaty of eighteen hundred and five; six hundred dollars per annum for the support of light horsemen, under the thirteenth article of the treaty of eighteen hundred and twenty; permanent annuity of six thousand dollars for education, under the second article of the treaty of eighteen hundred and twenty-five; six hundred dollars per annum, permanent provision for the support of a blacksmith, under the sixth article of the treaty of eighteen hundred and twenty; and three hundred and twenty dollars, permanent provision for iron and steel, under the ninth article of the treaty of eighteen hundred and twenty-five—shall continue to be paid to, or expended for the benefit of, the Choctaws as heretofore, or the same may be applied to such objects of general utility as may from time to time be designated by the general council of the tribe, with the approbation of the government of the United States. And the funds now held in trust by the United States for the benefit of the Choctaws under former treaties, or otherwise, shall continue to be so held; together with the sum of five hundred thousand dollars out of the amount payable to them under articles eighth and tenth of this agreement, and also whatever balance shall remain, if any, of the amount that shall be allowed the Choctaws by the Senate, under the twelfth article hereof, after satisfying the just liabilities of the tribe. The sums so to be held in trust shall constitute a general Choctaw fund, yielding an annual interest of not less than five per centum; no part of which shall be paid out as annuity, but shall be regularly and judiciously applied, under the direction of the general council of the Choctaws, to the support of their government, for purposes of education, and such other objects as may be best calculated to promote and advance the improvement, welfare and happiness of the Choctaw people and their descendants.

"ARTICLE XIV. The United States shall protect the Choctaws and Chickasaws from domestic strife, from hostile invasion, and from aggression by other Indians and white persons not subject to their jurisdiction and laws; and for all injuries, resulting from such invasion or aggression, full indemnity is hereby guarantied to the party or parties injured, out of the treasury of the United States, upon the same principle and according to the same rules upon which white persons are entitled to indemnity for injuries or aggressions upon them committed by Indians.

"ARTICLE XV. The Choctaws and Chickasaws shall promptly apprehend and deliver up all persons accused of any crime or offence against the laws of the United States, or of any State thereof, who may be found within their limits, on demand of any proper officer of a State, or of the United States.

"ARTICLE XVI. All persons licensed by the United States to trade with the Choctaws or Chickasaws, shall be required to pay to the respective tribes a moderate annual compensation for the land and timber used by them; the amount of such compensation, in each case, to be assessed by the proper authorities of said tribe, subject to the approval of the United States agent.

"ARTICLE XVII. The United States shall have the right to establish and maintain such military posts, post roads, and Indian agencies, as may be deemed necessary within the Choctaw and Chickasaw country, but no greater quantity of land or timber shall be used for said purposes than shall be actually requisite; and if, in the establishment or maintenance of such posts, post roads, and agencies, the property of any Choctaw or Chickasaw shall be taken, injured or destroyed, just and adequate compensation shall be made by the United States. Only such persons as are or may be in the employment of the United States, or subject to the jurisdiction and laws of the Choctaws or Chickasaws, shall be permitted to farm or raise stock within the limits of any of said military posts or Indian agencies. And no offender against the laws of either of said tribes shall be permitted to take refuge therein.

"ARTICLE XVIII. The United States, or any incorporated company, shall have the right of way for railroads, or lines of telegraphs, through the Choctaw and Chickasaw country; but for any property taken or destroyed in the construction thereof, full compensation shall be made to the party or parties injured, to be ascertained and determined in such manner as the President of the United States shall direct.

"ARTICLE XIX. The United States shall, as soon as practicable, cause the eastern and western boundary lines of the tract of country described in the 1st article of this convention, and the western boundary of the Chickasaw district, as herein defined, to be run and permanently marked.

"ARTICLE XX. That this convention may conduce as far as possible to the restoration and preservation of kind and friendly feeling among the Choctaws and Chickasaws, a general amnesty of all past offences, committed within their country, is hereby declared.

"And in order that their relations to each other and to the United States may hereafter be conducted in a harmonious and satisfactory manner, there shall be but one agent for the two tribes.

"ARTICLE XXI. This convention shall supersede and take the place of all former treaties between the United States and the Choctaws, and, also, of all treaty stipulations between the United States and the Chickasaws, and between the Choctaws and Chickasaws, inconsistent with this agreement, and shall take effect and be obligatory upon the contracting parties, from the date hereof, whenever the same shall be ratified by the respective councils of the Choctaw and Chickasaw tribes, and by the President and Senate of the United States.

"ARTICLE XXII. It is understood and agreed that the expenses of the respective commissioners of the two tribes, signing these articles of agreement and convention, in coming to, and returning from this city, and while here, shall be paid by the United States.

"In testimony whereof, the said George W. Manypenny, Commissioner on the part of the United States, and the said Commissioners on the part of the Choctaws and of the Chickasaws, have hereunto set their hands and seals.

"Done in triplicate, at the city of Washington, on this twenty-second day of June, in the year of our Lord one thousand eight hundred and fifty-five.

"GEORGE W. MANYPENNY, [L. S.]
United States Commissioner.
P. P. PITCHLYNN, [L. S.]
ISRAEL FOLSOM, [L. S.]
SAMUEL GARLAND, [L. S.]
DICKSON W. LEWIS, [L. S.]
Choctaw Commisioners.
EDMUND PICKENS, his × mark, [L. S.]
SAMPSOM FOLSOM, [L. S.]
Chickasaw Commissioners.

"Executed in the presence of—
A. O. P. Nicholson,
James G. Berrett,
Douglas H. Cooper, *United States Indian Agent.*

And whereas, the said treaty having been submitted to the general council of the Chickasaw tribe, the general council did, on the third day of October, A. D. one thousand eight hundred and fifty-five, assent to, ratify, and confirm the same, with the following amendment: "Add to the 19th article, By Commissioners to be appointed by the contracting parties hereto" by an instrument in writing, in the words and figures following, to wit:

"Whereas, articles of agreement and convention were made and concluded on the twenty-second day of June, A. D. one thousand eight hundred and fifty-five, by and between George W. Manypenny, Commissioner on the part of the United States; Peter P. Pitchlynn, Israel Folsom, Samuel Garland, and Dickson W. Lewis, Commissioners on the part of the Choctaws; and Edmund Pickens, and Sampsom Folsom, Commissioners on the part of the Chickasaws, at the city of Washington, in the District of Columbia, the preamble whereof is in the words and figures following, to wit: 'Whereas, the political connection heretofore existing between the Choctaw and Chickasaw tribes of Indians has given rise to unhappy and injurious dissensions and controversies among them, which render necessary a readjustment of their relations to each other and to the United States; and whereas, the United States desire that the Choctaw Indians shall relinquish all claim to any territory west of the one hundredth degree of west longitude, and also to make provision for the permanent settlement within the Choctaw country of the Wichita and certain other tribes or bands of Indians, for which purpose the Choctaws and Chickasaws are willing to lease, on reasonable terms, to the United States, that portion of their common territory which is west of the ninety-eighth degree of west longitude; and whereas, the Choctaws contend that, by a just and fair construction of the treaty of September 27, 1830, they are of right entitled to the nett proceeds of the lands ceded by them to the United States under said treaty, and have proposed that the question of their right to the same, together with the whole subject-matter of their unsettled claims, whether national or individual, against the United States, arising under the various provisions of said treaty, shall be referred to the Senate of the United States for final adjudication and adjustment; and whereas, it is necessary, for the simplification and better understanding of the relations between the United States and the Choctaw Indians, that all their subsisting treaty stipulations be embodied in one comprehensive instrument;' and whereas, in the twenty-first article thereof, it is, among other things, recited that said agreement 'shall take effect and be obligatory upon the contracting parties from the date hereof, whenever the same shall be ratified by the respective councils of the Choctaw and Chickasaw tribes of Indians and by the President and Senate of the United States.'

"Now, therefore, be it known, that the Chickasaws, in general council assembled, having duly considered said articles of agreement and convention, and each and every clause thereof, and being satisfied therewith, do, upon their part, hereby assent to, ratify, and confirm the same, as stipulated and required, with the following amendment: 'Add to the nineteenth article, By commissioners to be appointed by the contracting parties hereto.'

"Done and approved at Tishomingo, in the Chickasaw district of the Choctaw nation, this third day of October, in the year of our Lord one thousand eight hundred and fifty-five.

"Passed the Council.

JOEL KEMP, *President.*
D. COLBERT, *F. C.*

"Attest: CYRUS HARRIS, *Clerk of the Council.*"

And whereas the Chickasaws, in general council assembled, did, on the 13th day of December, A. D. 1855, recede from and rescind the said amendment, and did ratify and confirm the said treaty, and every part thereof, by an instrument in writing, in the words and figures following, to wit:

"Whereas the Chickasaws, in general council assembled, after having duly considered the stipulations contained in a certain convention and agreement, made and entered into at the city of Washington, on the 22d day of June, A. D. 1855, between George W. Manypenny, Commissioner on the part of the United States; Peter P. Pitchlynn, Israel Folsom, Samuel Garland, and Dickson W. Lewis, Commissioners on the part of the Choctaws; Edmund Pickens and Sampson Folsom, Commissioners on the part of the Chickasaws, did, on the third day of October, A. D. 1855, at Tishomingo, in the Chickasaw district, Choctaw Nation, assent to, ratify, and confirm each and every part of said convention and agreement, with the following amendment, viz: 'Add to the 19th article, By Commissioners to be appointed by the contracting parties hereto.' And whereas, said amendment was not duly considered and concurred in by the Choctaws in general council assembled; but said agreement and convention, and every part thereof, was assented to, ratified, and confirmed by said council without amendment. Now, therefore, be it known, that the Chickasaws, in general council assembled, having reconsidered said proposed amendment, do hereby recede from, and rescind the same, hereby assenting to, ratifying, and confirming said agreement and convention, and every part thereof.

"Done and approved at the council house at Tishomingo, Chickasaw district, Choctaw Nation, this 13th day of December, A. D. 1855.

"Approved, December 13, 1855.

J. McCOY, *President of the Council.*
DOUGHERTY COLBERT, *F. C.*

"Attest: Cyrus Harris, *Secretary.*

"Signed in presence of—
Jackson Frazier, *Chief Chickasaw district, Choctaw Nation.*
Douglas H. Cooper, *U. S. Indian Agent.*"

And whereas the said treaty having been submitted to the General Council of the Choctaw tribe, the said General Council did, on the 16th day of November, A. D. one thousand eight hundred and fifty-five, consent to and ratify the same by an instrument in the words and figures following, to wit:

"Whereas articles of agreement and convention were made and concluded on the twenty-second day of June, A. D. one thousand eight hundred and fifty-five, by and between George W. Manypenny, Commissioner on the part of the United States; Peter P. Pitchlynn, Israel Folsom, Samuel Garland, and Dickson W. Lewis, Commissioners on the part of the Choctaws; and Edmund Pickens and Sampson Folsom, Commissioners on the part of the Chickasaws, at the city of Washington, in the District of Columbia, the preamble whereof is in the words and figures following, viz: 'Whereas the political connexion heretofore existing between the Choctaw and the Chickasaw tribes of Indians has given rise to unhappy and injurious dissensions and controversies among them, which render necessary a readjustment of their relations to each other and to the United States; and whereas, the United States desire that the Choctaw Indians shall relinquish all claim to any territory west of the one hundredth degree of west longitude, and, also, to make provision for the permanent settlement within the Choctaw country, of the Wichita and certain other tribes or bands of Indians, for which purpose the Choctaws and Chickasaws are willing to lease, on reasonable terms, to the United States, that portion of their common territory which is west of the ninety-eighth degree of west longitude; and whereas, the Choctaws contend that, by a just and fair construction of the treaty ot September 27, 1830, they are of right entitled to the nett proceeds of the lands ceded by them to the United States under said treaty, and have proposed that the question of their right to the same, together with the whole subject matter of their unsettled claims, whether national or individual, against the United States, arising under the various provisions of said treaty, shall be referred to the Senate of the United States for final adjudication and adjustment; and whereas it is necessary, for the simplification and better understanding of the relations between the United States and the Choctaw Indians, that all their subsisting treaty stipulations be embodied in one comprehensive instrument;' and whereas, in the twenty-first article thereof, it is, among other things, recited that said agreement 'shall take effect and be obligatory upon the contracting parties from the date hereof, whenever the same shall be ratified by the respective councils of the Choctaw and Chickasaw tribes and by the President and Senate of the United States.'

"Now, therefore, be it known, that the Choctaws, in general council assembled, having duly considered said articles of agreement and convention, and each and every clause thereof, and being satisfied therewith, do, upon their part, hereby assent to, ratify and confirm the same as stipulated and required.

"Done and approved at the Council House, at Fort Towson, in the Choctaw Nation, this sixteenth day of November, in the year of our Lord one thousand eight hundred and fifty-five.

TANDY WALKER, *President of the Senate.*
KENNEDY M. CURTAIN, *Speaker of the House of Representatives.*

"Approved:

GEO. W. HARKINS, *Chief of Ahpuck District.*
N. COCHNANER, *Chief of Pushemathan District.*
ADAM CHRISTY, *Speaker and Acting Chief of Moosholatubbee District.*

"Signed in presence of—

DOUGLAS H. COOPER, *U. S. Indian Agent for Choctaw Tribe.*"

And whereas the said treaty having been submitted to the Senate of the United States for its constitutional action thereon, the Senate did, on the twenty-first day of February, A. D. one thousand eight hundred and fifty-six, advise and consent to the ratification of the same, by a resolution in the words and figures following, to wit:

"IN EXECUTIVE SESSION, SESSION OF THE UNITED STATES, February 21, 1856.

"*Resolved*, (two-thirds of the senators present concurring,) That the Senate advise and consent to the ratification of the articles of agreement and convention between the United States and the Choctaw and Chickasaw tribes of Indians, made and concluded at the city of Washington, the twenty-second day of June, Anno Domini one thousand eight hundred and fifty-five, by George W. Manypenny, commissioner on the part of the United States; Peter P. Pitchlynn, Israel Folsom, Samuel Garland, and Dixon W. Lewis, commissioners on the part of the Choctaws; and Edmund Pickens and Sampson Folsom, commissioners on the part of the Chickasaws.

"Attest:

ASBURY DICKINS, *Secretary.*"

Now, therefore, be it known, that I, Franklin Pierce, President of the United States of America, do, in pursuance of the advice and consent of the Senate, as expressed in their resolution of the twenty-first day of February, one thousand eight hundred and fifty-six, accept, ratify and confirm the said treaty.

In testimony whereof, I have caused the seal of the United States to be hereto affixed, having signed the same with my hand.

Done at the city of Washington, this fourth day of March, A. D. one thousand eight hundred and fifty-six, and of the independence of the United States the eightieth.

[L. S.]

FRANKLIN PIERCE.

By the President:

W. L. Marcy, *Secretary of State.*

INDEX.

CONSTITUTION, ACTS, AND JOINT RESOLUTIONS.

APPENDIX.